LIVE WITHOUT ANXIETY

The Most Effective Method to Stop Overthinking, Overcome Stress, Declutter your Mind and Achieve Inner Peace and Happiness

Jesús Cediel

JCM PRODUCTIONS

Disclaimer:

This book is designed to provide readers with motivation and information. The author does not offer psychological, legal, medical, or any other form of professional advice or treatment. The content is not intended to replace professional medical advice but solely represents the author's opinions and expressions. No express or implied guarantee is made by the author or publisher regarding the content of the book. Neither the publisher nor the author shall be held responsible for any physical, psychological, emotional, financial, or commercial damages resulting from the use of the book's content. Readers are explicitly advised to consult qualified medical professionals before undertaking any actions based on the content.

Contents

THE ROOT OF THE PROBLEM

"The man who masters his mind can conquer anything."
D.T. Suzuki

THE SAMURAI UNSHEATHED HIS katana with a harmonious motion. Its edge gleamed under the sun. With great precision, his tense arms executed a sequence of slashes and thrusts into the air. Each movement was perfect, fluid, and unwavering. The sword whistled, cutting through the wind.

Suddenly, the warrior pivoted on his heels, his breathing steady. In one final movement, the katana cleaved a leaf into two perfect halves before it was returned to its sheath. The samurai remained motionless, his focus unshakable.

Have you ever wondered if you would feel less stressed if your mind followed all of your instructions? Imagine for a moment that you could tell your mind not to worry about imaginary situations or overthink, and it would obey without interruption. Do you think you would suffer from anxiety then?

The answer is simple and unequivocal: no.

What happens if your body and mind are out of control and do not follow your directions? In that case, they have rebelled against you and taken command.

It is true that genetic and social factors influence anxiety. There are even triggering situations that can spike your stress levels. Some people think they are this way because their father or grandfather suffered from anxiety, too. They believe it is inevitable that they, too, will suffer from anxiety, that it is in their genes, and that they can't do anything about it.

However, these justifications do not offer real solutions. They are an example of the type of limiting thinking that ensures you remain trapped in a dreamlike fantasy that will not help you escape the problem. The truth is you can't turn back time and change the past, nor can you transform your father or grandfather. But what you can do is transform your present situation if you set your mind to it. You just need to know how to do so.

So, why do you search for solutions in the wrong place?

The first step is to recognize that you are not presently capable of controlling your mind as you wish. That's the key to it all: your psycho-physical system is designed in such a way that you need to learn how to use it properly. Just like when you use an air conditioner, if you don't know how it works, you won't be able to benefit from it, and it could even harm you if you misuse it. You need to read and understand the instruction manual in order to get the most out of it.

Here's another analogy: Picture your mind as a sharp knife. If you are not careful when you use it, you might cut yourself. But ask yourself this: If that were to happen, would it be the knife's fault or the lack of steadiness in the hand holding it?

The knife can be a destructive or constructive tool, depending on how you use it. The same happens with your mind: you have the amazing ability to think, but without a stable mental framework, this ability can cause you to become emotionally overwhelmed. Therefore, the sharper and keener your mind is, the greater the damage you can cause if you don't handle it with firmness and balance. That is to say, your intellect is a powerful tool but wielded recklessly, and it can cut like a double-edged sword, hurting both yourself and those around you.

The solution does not lie in "dulling" your intellect by resorting to taking sedatives to alleviate stress and anxiety. What you need is to give your mind stability, which is equivalent to strengthening the hand so that it is steady when it wields the knife.

That's what this book is about. Throughout these pages, I will provide you with the instruction manual you need to understand and manage your mind.

Just as a samurai perfects his technique with constant practice, you, too, can learn to master your mind and emotions.

I will give you practical and simple tools to help you learn how to stabilize your thoughts and emotions so that you can make the most of your mental potential without falling into the dangers of overthinking and anxiety. Once you achieve that mental stability, the rest will come. You will be able to focus your mind on achieving your goals, solving problems, and enjoying life with fullness and satisfaction.

LIGHT THE WICK

The Power of Reinvention

WELCOME TO YOUR NEW life! No matter what obstacles you faced in the past, your future is a blank page ready to be written by you. It's time to reinvent yourself and become the person you want to be. Every day is an opportunity to start over, to choose your identity, and to define who you will be and what you will become from this day forward. You have the power to take control of your destiny and create the life you have always dreamed of. Don't let fear or doubt stop you. Trust in your ability to overcome challenges and achieve your most ambitious goals. You are stronger and more capable than you might believe you are, so embrace your unlimited potential and take the first step toward a bright future full of possibilities. The path to becoming your best self begins here and now.

Do you know why some people learn and grow faster than others? The answer is simple. They are people who take action; they DO instead of just reading books or watching videos online. They don't just wait for things to happen; they take control of their own learning and growth. So, if you would like to join that group of people, it's time for you to start DOING. Don't settle for being a spectator; become the protagonist of your own personal growth.

Remember when you were a kid and you learned to ride a bicycle? You didn't do it by reading a book about bikes, did you? No, of course, you didn't. You learned by riding and practicing, by daring to get on that bike again and again, no matter how many times you fell off. You pushed your-self out of your comfort zone by failing and coming home with skinned knees, but that didn't stop you. Undeterred, you kept trying until you could finally keep your balance and pedal on your own.

The same is true when it comes to learning a skill or implementing a new habit in your life that will allow you to overcome anxiety. You can't just read about it and, without taking action, expect it to magically happen to you. You have to put in the work and practice and be willing to make mistakes along the way.

It's not that there's anything wrong with reading books; in fact, it's a great way to gain knowledge and new perspectives. But if you don't put it into practice, if you don't put what you learn into action, it's the same as nothing.

If you want to change your life and overcome anxiety, don't just read. Take action.

In 2023, when Spanish coach Luis Lafuente Castillo took over the Spanish national soccer team during transition, he made the following statements at a press conference: "There is always room for improvement in every-thing. We have to get better every day. The next objective is these two games, and we want to win both to finish first in the group. I thank the players at the end of training, but I also tell them there is room for improvement. I warn them it won't be easy. It will take discipline, patience and perseverance. But rest assured, the results will come."

With these words, a clear vision, and renewed commitment, Luis Lafuente expressed his confidence and determination to lead the team to new levels of success. It was the beginning of one of the most fruitful moments for the Spanish national football team, which culminated in winning the Euro Nations Cup in July 2024.

This period was not only a series of victories on the pitch but also a transformation in the team's mentality. It is a clear testimony that with vision, commitment and constant effort, you can achieve any goal you set your mind to.

So, what are you waiting for? It's time to take control and create the life you really want. Go ahead, the future is here!

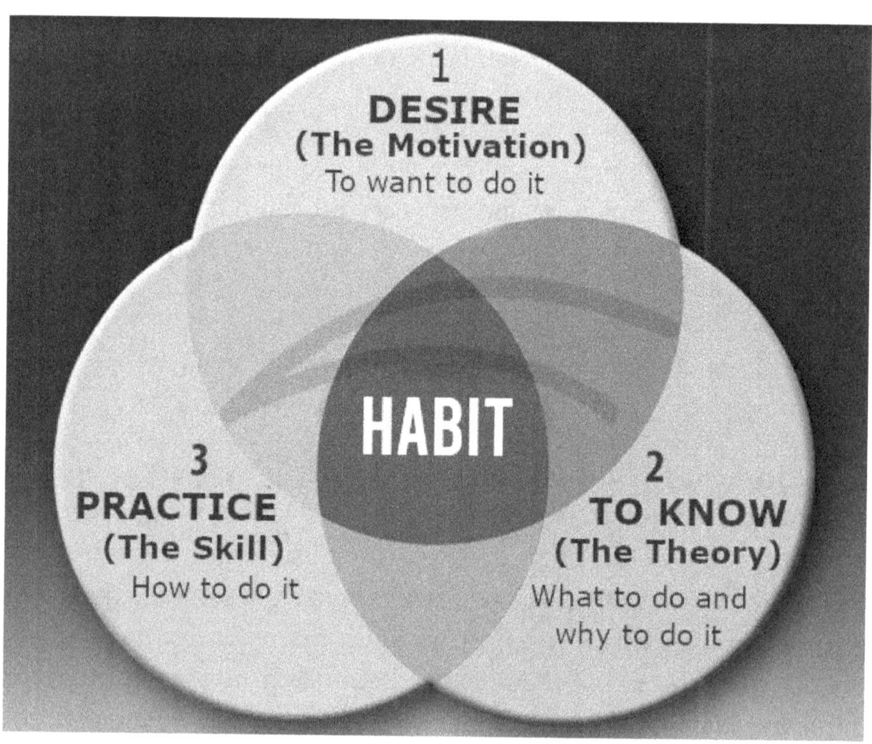

CONSCIOUSNESS AND ENERGY

You are about to embark on an exciting journey of personal transformation. For this, I have divided this journey into two blocks: **Awareness (Understanding)** and **Energy (Action)**.

The first block, **Understanding,** is the theoretical foundation, while the second, **Action,** is where you will put what you have learned into practice. Both are essential and complement each other for the best results.

Why this structure? Simple. To take actions that will improve your life, you must first be convinced of their effectiveness. Only then will you be able to carry them out with the energy and determination necessary to achieve success.

So the book is split into two halves. In the first part, called **Awareness**, you will find the knowledge you need to act on a solid foundation. You will learn who you are and how your mind works. You will also learn about powerful tools and why they are effective.

The second part, called **Energy**, is where the action comes in. Here, you will put these tools into practice and apply everything you have learned in the first part with determination.

Think of your energy as an inner fire sleeping within you, waiting to be awakened. When you learn to ignite it and direct it with knowledge, you can accomplish great things.

Eastern traditions know the mystery of creation. In Hinduism, the Goddess Shakti symbolises energy and is represented by a serpent called Kundalini, who sleeps at the base of the spine in the root chakra. At the same time, her lover, the god Shiva, who symbolizes consciousness, also sleeps at the crown of the head in the seventh chakra.

According to this beautiful story, Shakti (energy) awakens and begins to dance to awaken Shiva (consciousness). Through the love of her dance, she causes Shiva to open his eyes and join her in the dance. The two gods merge into one being through their affection. These are the mystical weddings where male and female, consciousness and energy, unite to give birth to a new being.

What does this story mean to you? It means your task is to learn to awaken and direct your energy with the light of your consciousness. How do you do this? Through the tools and exercises, you will learn in this book. Little by little, you will ignite the inner fire that will propel you toward your goals with passion and determination.

The two parts of this book, **Awareness** and **Energy**, are like germ cells that will unite to give life to a new being. A new, happier and fearless version of you will be born from this union.

By combining consciousness and energy, you will act like a farmer who fertilizes a seed with water and light, and plant that seed in the fertile soil of your mind. With every positive thought and decisive action, you are watering that seed with the water of your will. Day by day, with consistency and dedication, you will see that seed germinate, take root, and become a strong and vigorous plant.

MODULE I

AWARENESS

CHAPTER 1

What Is Anxiety and What Is Its Origin?

"People are generally better persuaded by the reasons which they have themselves discovered than by those which have come into the mind of others."

Blaise Pascal (1623–1662)

JOHN ARRIVES AT HIS office early. As he sits down at his desk and looks at the pile of papers and unread emails that have accumulated since the previous day, he feels his heart begin to race. He knows he has several important meetings scheduled for today, including a crucial presentation to his boss and key investors from a foreign company.

He begins to feel anxious as he scans his calendar. Dark thoughts haunt him: Have I adequately prepared for this meeting? What if I forget important points during the presentation? He begins to imagine the worst-case scenarios: being ridiculed in front of everyone, losing the respect of his boss, even risking his job.

John tries to focus on his responsibilities, but his mind continues to race with worry. He feels a knot in his stomach and finds it hard to breathe. Every time his phone rings, or he receives a new email, he jumps for fear of more problems or impossible demands.

As the hours go by, John's anxiety increases. He wonders if he is doing enough, or if he is good enough at his job. He obsessively reviews his notes for the presentation, unable to shake the feeling that he is missing something.

When the big meeting arrives, John is on the verge of a panic attack. His hands feel shaky, and a cold sweat runs down his back as he sets up the projector. When he begins to speak, his voice shakes slightly, and he worries that everyone will notice his nervousness.

Although he has prepared thoroughly for the presentation, John cannot help but feel that he is failing, that he is not measuring up. Every question from the clients feels like a personal challenge. By the end of the meeting, he feels mentally and physically exhausted.

Back at his desk, John sinks into his chair, feeling overwhelmed and defeated, even though the presentation, despite a few setbacks, went reasonably well. He knows his anxiety is irrational, but he cannot stop it from affecting every aspect of his working day. He wonders how much longer he can go on like this, trapped in this endless cycle of worry and self-criticism.

The Epidemic of Overthinking: A Modern Concern

Today, no one is safe from one of the great epidemics of modern society: the lack of control over the mind and thoughts. We live in a fast-paced world full of constant stimuli, limitless information, and endless demands. No wonder so many people feel overwhelmed and trapped in an endless cycle of stress and anxiety.

The term "overthinking" has become an increasingly common way of describing the tendency to obsessively contemplate and incessantly repeat thought patterns that lead to a vicious cycle of stress, anxiety, nervousness and self-doubt.

The Dictionary of the Royal Spanish Academy defines anxiety as "a state of agitation, restlessness, or fear of the mind. Its synonyms include anxiety, restlessness, uneasiness, and worry" (Real Academia Española, n.d.). The same dictionary is more specific in its medical definition, describing "anxiety" as "a fear that often accompanies various diseases, especially certain neuroses, and that disturbs the peace of mind of those who suffer from it."

But what about the impact of anxiety and stress on your life and, more importantly, how do you free yourself from its clutches? This book will help you there. You will learn practical and effective strategies to stop overthinking and regain control of your mind. No matter how long you've struggled with anxiety, there is hope. With the right approach and tools, you can transform your relationship with your thoughts and create a calmer, more satisfying life for yourself.

Have you ever felt overwhelmed by life's uncertainties? Have you experienced that uneasy feeling that takes over your mind in everyday situations? It's important to realize that any situation you face on a daily basis can create an emotional state of mental upset or stress. Basically, because the outcome of any event in life is more or less uncertain, anxiety can take over your mind.

Think about when you are late for a work appointment, waiting for the results of medical tests, or getting on a plane to go on a trip. The anxiety you might feel is completely normal. After all, you are a tiny being in the vastness of the universe, and you have no absolute certainty about how events will unfold in the future.

Recognizing that some degree of anxiety is a natural response is the first step to dealing with anxiety effectively. There is nothing pathological about feeling a certain amount of it in the face of the unknown. In fact, a little anxiety can be beneficial because it keeps you alert and spurs you to action.

For some people, however, anxiety is an unwanted constant companion. They wake up with a feeling of nervousness for no apparent reason that follows them throughout the day, a kind of perpetual restlessness that prevents them from enjoying life. It can even interfere with sleep quality, causing disturbances that compound the problem.

Anxiety might also be a consequence of their preoccupation with specific issues: recurring thoughts that seem to have a life of their own and that, like a broken record, play over and over in their minds, tormenting them incessantly.

Recognizing Normal vs. Pathological Anxiety

So, when does anxiety become a pathological disorder? The answer depends largely on the subjective judgment of the diagnosing physician. No clear and defined line separates normal anxiety from pathological anxiety.

Imagine going to your doctor. According to the diagnostic criteria, to be diagnosed with generalized anxiety disorder, you must have "markedly excessive worry and anxiety about a wide range of everyday topics, events, or activities. And this must have been going on for at least six months in a row."

But how does the doctor determine that your worry has crossed the threshold from normal to excessive? At what exact point is it decided that you need professional help? Well, there is no single, definitive answer. Each professional will use his or her own criteria and experience to evaluate your particular case.

These range from specific phobias, such as an irrational fear of ants, to obsessive-compulsive disorder (OCD), which is characterized by intrusive, repetitive thoughts (obsessions) leading to compulsive behaviors, such as excessive hand washing or repeatedly checking if the door is locked. They also include generalized anxiety disorder (GAD), which involves excessive worry about everyday issues.

Now, does it really matter what the exact name of the disorder you are diagnosed with is? After all, the label doesn't change the reality of what you're experiencing. And it doesn't get to the root of the problem.

So, what is anxiety, and what causes it? Most people believe that their anxiety stems from their thoughts. That's why the majority of anxiety-relief therapies focus on changing those thoughts to reduce symptoms.

However, I am going to reveal a truth that will change your perspective: the origin of anxiety is not your thoughts, even though they are intimately connected. Anxiety comes from an emotion.

Think about it: two people can face the same situation and react in entirely different ways. One may be filled with fear, while the other remains calm. The difference is in their emotional processes.

So what are emotions? They are not just abstract ideas floating around in your head. Emotions are actually your brain's subjective interpretations of the sensory data it receives from the various organs in your body. This process is known in modern neuroscience as "interoception."

What really causes your anxiety is not the external situations themselves but rather, it's your way of perceiving and interpreting them. How you interpret your thoughts is what creates those overwhelming emotions and unpleasant physical sensations.

Traditional medicine often focuses on the outward symptoms of anxiety, which can be numerous and varied. However, the true cause of anxiety is unique and lies within you.

Your mind is the key to the anxiety process. Some people feel that their mind is constantly looking for reasons to feel anxious, and they are right. The situations or objects around you are just excuses that your mind uses to create this internal tension.

For an artist, standing in front of a blank canvas can be like standing before a portal to a universe of infinite possibilities. But for an individual with an uncontrolled mind, that same canvas becomes a source of stress. For an adventurer who longs to spend a weekend exploring unknown lands, uncertainty is exciting and desirable. But to someone who constantly seeks security, this lack of certainty creates anxiety. All of this can be exacerbated when excessive, unchannelled nervous tension materializes into a panic attack. You find yourself trapped in a vicious cycle where the fear not only remains in your mind but also manifests itself physically. Your body cries out for help, every muscle tense, every breath strained.

The Nature of Anxiety: Causes and Perceptions

Picture this: you're sitting at home; everything seems normal, but suddenly, unexpectedly, you feel the world crumbling around you. Every heartbeat thunders in your ears like war drums. Your hands sweat, your chest tightens, and you feel suffocated.

"What's happening to me?" you ask yourself as fear grips you.

The first time someone has an anxiety attack, it's hard to recognize.

Help, I can't breathe! you think.

Your mind runs wild, searching for explanations. You might believe you are having a heart attack because the sensations you experience at that moment are so distressing. The feeling of loss of control is overwhelming, and every second seems eternal. You are afraid of dying, afraid of losing your mind.

Yet, it's important to remember that, although panic attacks are extremely uncomfortable and frightening, they are not fatal. What is happening is that your body is reacting to the extreme stress, and adrenaline is flooding your system like an unstoppable waterfall.

Yes, fear of losing control is a major cause of anxiety. Your mind is desperate to create a framework of security in your life, and it is its essential nature. It wants to control every aspect, every detail, to feel safe. But here's the great paradox: the more you try to control, the more out of control you create.

Imagine you are driving a car on a winding road. If you squeeze the wheel too hard, if you try to control every little movement and every curve, you will lose control of the car. On the other hand, if you relax and allow the car to flow naturally along the road, you will maintain greater control.

The same is true with your mind. When you seek excessive control, when you cling desperately to the idea of security, you create the exact opposite: lack of control. That lack of control manifests as emotional imbalance, anxiety and stress.

According to Aristotle, virtue lies in finding a moderate position between two extremes—excess and deficiency. The point is not to give up control altogether but to find a healthy middle ground. Too much control is just as harmful as a total lack of control. Too much control is an illusion that only takes you away from your well-being.

Simultaneously, stress is like a snowball that grows and grows, feeding itself in a vicious cycle. Once you're in that cycle, it's difficult to get out.

Pay close attention to what I'm about to tell you: **anxiety is an addiction, just like smoking or any other addiction.** That may sound strange, but it's true. Your brain becomes addicted to the chemicals that are released during episodes of anxiety. This is because when you are anxious, your body releases adrenaline and cortisol, the stress hormones. At first, these hormones give you an energy boost and make you feel alert and alive. This is part of the fight-or-flight response. But over time, because your brain is releasing so much of these chemicals, it begins to crave this feeling; it starts looking for reasons to feel anxious just to get that chemical high.

It's comparable to a smoker who lights up cigarette after cigarette. They know it's not good for their health, but they can't help it.

The same thing happens with fear. The more anxiety you feel, the more your brain craves that feeling. It becomes a feedback loop where anxiety feeds more anxiety.

But here's the good news: just as it's possible to break a cigarette addiction, it's also possible to break the anxiety cycle. With the right strategies and tools, you can retrain your brain to seek calm instead of chaos.

The solution to treating anxiety and overthinking is easier than you might think. You don't need magic pills or endless therapy. Everything you need is right here, in the pages of this book, where you will find practical and effective tools to calm your mind and regain the inner peace you crave. Proven strategies that have helped countless people overcome anxiety and regain control of their lives.

It's up to you to take the first step. You have the power to change your life. If you think you can, you're right. And if you think you can't, you're right, too. Your mind is incredibly powerful. What you believe is what you create.

I have seen this principle in action time and time again. People come to me in despair, convinced that they can never change. But instead of giving up, they choose to act. They take the first courageous step toward change. And little by little, their lives begin to change.

The truth is, you are the architect of your own life. You build it brick by brick with your thoughts, beliefs, emotions, and actions. Your mind is the crucible in which all these elements merge to form your reality.

If you fill that crucible with thoughts of fear and doubt, that is what will manifest in your life. But if you fill it with thoughts of calm, courage and infinite possibility, that is what you will create.

The choice is yours. You can choose to remain trapped in the cycle of fear, or you can choose to break free. You can choose to remain a victim of your thoughts, or you can choose to be the master of your mind. After all, your mind is an incredibly powerful tool. You can learn to train it to work for you, to bring you the things you want, and to help you deal with the things you can't control.

I have dedicated my life to the study of the human mind. Since the age of 14, I have sought to understand how the human mind works and how we can harness its full potential. In the pages of this book, I have simply and effectively structured the strategies and tools that will help you achieve the peace of mind and spiritual peace you crave. But you must commit to the process. Reading this book is not a passive exercise. It is an invitation to action, to transformation. If you are serious about reading it and putting it into practice, you can be sure that you will open a door that will change your life forever.

This is not a religious book, although we will explore the spiritual nature of the human being. The truth is that you are much more than a physical body. You are a being of infinite energy and potential. And when you learn to align your mind, body, and spirit, you will become unstoppable.

In the pages of this book, you will find not only theoretical principles that will help you understand things but also practical tools that will allow you to experience the truth of these principles in your own life.

Do not underestimate the power of these tools because of their apparent simplicity. The great truths of life are simple, but human ignorance often tries to hide them under complicated formulas. If you have the limiting belief that great truths are difficult to express and understand, it's time to get rid of it. In fact, it is just the opposite: be suspicious when someone explains something poorly understood.

Remember, you can create big changes in your existence with small actions. You don't have to make drastic or overwhelming changes to transform your life. Every small step in the right direction brings you closer to the life you want.

Think of your life as a big jigsaw puzzle. Every action, every thought and every belief you hold is a piece of the puzzle. You may sometimes feel that the pieces are scattered and don't make sense, but as you apply the principles and tools in this book, the pieces will begin to fit together.

Gradually, the picture of your life will become clearer. You will begin to see patterns and connections that were previously unnoticed, and you will realize that you have more control over your life than you thought. This is a gradual process, but the results will be profound and lasting. When you change your mind, you change your life. As you adopt new beliefs and habits, you create a new reality.

Don't be discouraged if you don't see tangible results immediately. Remember, every great achievement begins with small steps. Just as the miracle of life begins with the union of two tiny cells, a sperm and an egg, and then requires a gestation period of about 9 months, the changes in your life will take some time to manifest.

If you make small positive changes in your daily routine and remain consistent, success will be yours. Significant changes will come in time. Keep the faith and the certainty that you are on the right path.

Do the exercises, practice the techniques, and introduce new habits into your life. I suggest that you read the book the first time with a pen and notebook handy to take notes if you wish. Then, read the book a second time and begin to make a plan. Pick some of the exercises that resonate with you the most and start incorporating new habits into your routine.

Congratulations! A journey of a thousand miles begins with a single step. And you've already taken that brave first step. Now, move forward with determination and persistence. The road to peace of mind and happiness lies before you. All you have to do is keep walking, one step at a time.

CHAPTER 2

The Human Being Is a Multidimensional Entity

"Happiness is when what you think, what you say and what you do are in harmony."

Mahatma Gandhi

THE ANCIENT TEMPLE STOOD *majestically among the mountains of Tibet, a silent witness to centuries of wisdom and tradition. It was here that monks would gather at dawn to begin their day, seeking enlightenment through meditation and study.*

Among them was a wise old man known as Master Tienzin. His understanding of human nature and his ability to guide the young monks on their spiritual path made him a respected and beloved figure to all.

One morning, as the sun began to peek out from behind the mountains, a young monk named Rinchen approached Master Tienzin. His face showed confusion.

With a gesture of reverence, Rinchen bowed to the Master and said, "Master, I am devoted to the practice of meditation and study, but I feel that something is missing. It is as if I am disconnected from a part of myself."

Master Tienzin had known Rinchen since he had entered the monastery as a child. With a gentle smile, Master Tienzin invited the young monk to sit next to him. The master spoke in a soft but firm voice. "Rinchen," he said, "the human being is like a mandala: it's composed of many layers and dimensions. Every tradition, whether spiritual or philosophical, teaches us that we are not simply a physical body but a harmonious integration of mind, spirit and emotions. Lack of balance in your life is the result of ignorance of these layers."

The young monk listened intently, absorbed in Master Tienzin's words. The old man continued, "In the ancient Hindu tradition, the human being is said to be made up of koshas, or sheaths, ranging from the physical body to the bliss body. In Buddhism, we speak of skandhas, or aggregates that make up our experience of life. Many Western philosophies recognize the importance of balancing body, mind and spirit. Rinchen, your journey to inner peace begins with understanding and integrating all parts of your being. Meditate on these teachings and enter into each dimension of your existence."

You Are a Multidimensional Being

This conversation between Rinchen and Master Tienzin illustrates a universal truth. Like the young monk, many of us seek answers in a world that often seems fragmented.

It is important for you to realize that you are a multidimensional being, made up of much more than your physical body. Although in your daily life, you may focus primarily on the material world that you perceive with your five senses, do not believe that there are no dimensions further beyond your usual perception.

According to various traditions, both Eastern and Western, each of us has different "bodies" or "vehicles" that operate at different vibrational frequencies. Imagine your being as an onion, with different layers or "bodies" operating at different vibrational frequencies. Each of these layers is interconnected; they exist in a different dimension. You may not be aware of it, but all the dimensions of this universe are intertwined and distinguished by their different wavelengths.

To better understand this concept, consider the analogy of tuning a radio. As you turn the dial, you change frequencies and listen to different channels. Countless radio channels are broadcasting their programs simultaneously; you just have to know how to tune in to hear the one you're looking for. Think of these radio frequencies as dimensions and your mind as the radio with which you connect to them.

However, your consciousness might be tuned to just one frequency. This is limiting your experience primarily to the three-dimensional or physical dimension. But ask yourself this: *what if I could expand my perception and access other dimensions of my being?*

Prepare for a remarkable revelation! You can! You can expand your consciousness and access dimensions beyond the physical. You are a multi-faceted being made up of physical, mental, emotional and spiritual aspects. You can tune into different frequencies like a radio and explore the different layers of your existence.

It's because you are like a quantum particle, capable of existing in multiple dimensions simultaneously. Although you may not be aware of it, you are experiencing this multidimensional reality right now!

As you delve into your deepest essence, you will discover that you are connected to a vast universe that transcends what you perceive with your senses. While fundamental to your experience on this earthly plane, your physical body is only a small part of the totality of your being.

I invite you to take a small detour that may seem like a departure from the main topic but is fundamental to understanding the nature of your being. When your physical body ceases to exist, your energy does not disappear but is transformed into other forms. Physical death is simply a transition, a change of state; your essence will continue to exist in other dimensions.

A fundamental law of physics states that energy is neither created nor destroyed, only transformed. This principle also applies to your being: death is not the end but a new beginning.

By understanding that death is an illusion, the first veil of Maya is lifted. Practices such as prolonged water fasting not only provide physical and mental benefits but also prepare you to understand this transition. During a prolonged fast, your body goes through a process similar to the agony of a dying person, allowing you to glimpse the illusory nature of death.

Your physical body is only the tip of the iceberg, the densest and most tangible manifestation of your being. Behind this material structure lies a complex energy web that supports and shapes your more material reality.

According to ancient yogic teachings, matter is nothing more than condensed energy vibrating at a lower frequency. This energy, in turn, results from the condensation of thought, mind, or spirit. In other words, you are a single element vibrating in different frequencies and dimensions.

Think of water in its three states: solid (ice), liquid (water), and gas (steam). Although its appearance and properties vary, its essence remains the same. Similarly, there is a common element in all manifestations of your existence, from your physical body to your more subtle, energetic body.

Your energetic form, which, according to the yogic tradition, is composed of chakras (energy centers), nadis (energy channels), and energetic bodies, acts as support for your physical body. It is the invisible scaffolding that supports and shapes your material structure.

In fact, diseases are first forged in your energetic form before they manifest in your physical body.

The Septenary Constitution of the Universe

Now, let's look at how different cultures have interpreted these concepts over time.

Ancient traditions, from the Vedas to the sacred books of Egypt, to the Upanishads, to the ancient texts of Zoroastrianism, and the Kabbalah, tell us about the number 7 and its importance in our lives. This mysterious number appears again and again, revealing its profound meaning.

Time itself is described as a shining wheel with seven spokes that carry you forward in your daily existence. Each spoke represents a world, a dimension of your being, and the central hub is immortality, the eternal essence that resides within you. As written in the Vedas:

"Time, like a chariot with seven wheels and seven hubs, marches onward; the swift wheels are all the worlds, its axle is immortality"

Atharva Veda (XIX, 53)

Notice these amazing synchronicities that will reveal to you the meaning of the number 7:

There are 7 days in a week and 52 weeks in a year (5 + 2 = 7).

- The ancient Mesopotamian creation epic, the *Enuma Elish*, divides creation into 7 clay tablets.

- The book of *Genesis*, inspired by the above work, tells us that the Earth was created in 7 days.

- Look around you: 7 colors make up the spectrum of the rainbow. When you listen to music, there are 7 notes that make up the melodies that move you.

- According to ancient traditions, your energy body comprises 7 chakras, or energy centers. And in the spiritual realm, they speak of the seven deadly sins and the seven virtues that guide your path.

- In China, 7 and 49 (7 x 7) are considered lucky numbers.

And let us not forget the words of Hippocrates, the father of medicine: *"The number 7, by its occult virtues, tends to realize all things; it is the dispenser of life and the source of all changes, for even the moon changes its phase every seven days: this number influences all exalted beings."*

Even in modern science, we find the presence of the number 7. Did you know that the periodic table of chemical elements is divided into 7 periods?

Amazing, isn't it? The number 7 is everywhere. Coincidence? Unlikely, because now you know why it's so special!

The Septenary Constitution of the Universe and the 7 Hermetic Principles offer us the key to understanding how the cosmos was formed and how it works.

The Septenary Constitution of the Universe suggests that everything is made up of 7 fundamental aspects or principles. It teaches that the universe is organized into distinct layers or dimensions that interact with one another. These layers range from the abstract and spiritual to the physical world. What brings them together is the notion of the interconnectedness of all existence. What happens in one layer can affect another, offering a deeper understanding of the cosmos!

On the other hand, the 7 Hermetic Principles offer a practical guide to understanding the universe's aspects, and are comprised of:

1. **The Principle of Mentalism**: The universe is a mental creation of a higher consciousness. Our thoughts shape our reality.

2. **The Principle of Correspondence**: "As above, so below." This highlights the connection between the macrocosm (the universe) and the microcosm (the individual), showing that similar laws operate at both levels.

3. **The Principle of Vibration**: Everything in the universe is in constant motion or vibration, with different forms of matter vibrating at different frequencies.

4. **The Principle of Polarity**: Everything has its opposite (e.g., light and darkness). This duality is crucial for understanding reality and how opposites are interdependent.

5. **The Principle of Rhythm**: The universe moves in cycles, creating patterns that govern the rise and fall of events. Recognizing these rhythms helps us navigate life's ups and downs.

6. **The Principle of Cause and Effect**: Nothing happens by chance; every cause has its effect. Understanding this empowers us to take responsibility for our actions.

7. **The Principle of Gender**: Gender exists in everything, manifesting as masculine and feminine energies that create and sustain life. This interplay fosters balance and harmony.

These principles reveal that the One Reality manifests in seven aspects, both in the cosmos and in you.

You are like a Russian nesting doll within 7 layers that intertwine and complement each other. Each of these layers, or dimensional vehicles, is essential to your personal development and growth.

In total, you possess 7 dimensional vehicles of different vibrations, each with specific characteristics and functions.

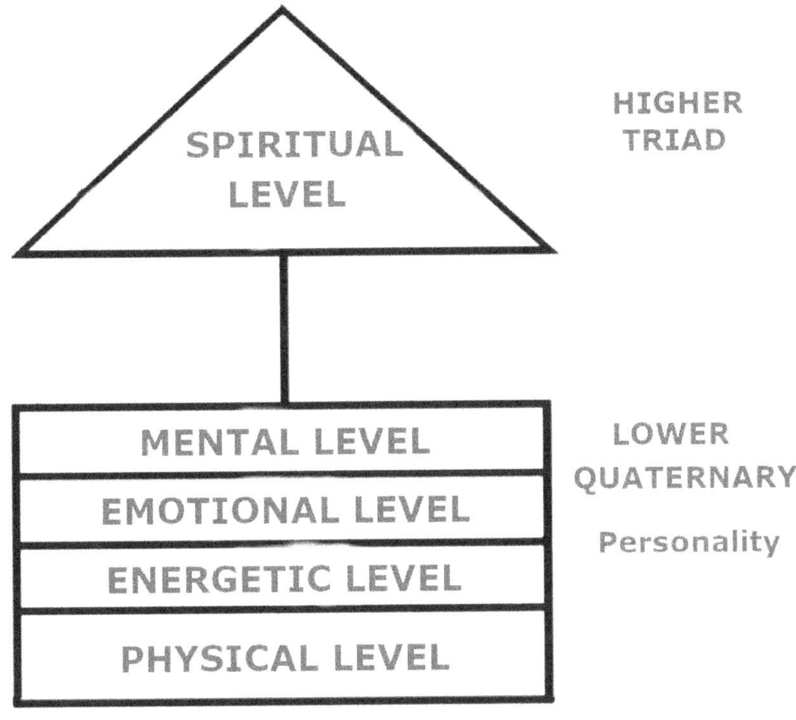

Let's begin with the densest and most tangible vehicle: your physical body. This is the sacred temple that houses your soul and allows you to move through this material world. It comprises the densest elements of creation: earth, water, fire, and air. But your physical body is just the tip of the iceberg. Behind it is your *pranic* or vital body, which acts as an energetic mold for your physical structure. This body is responsible for giving life to every cell of your being.

Next is your emotional or astral body, the home of your emotions and desires. This vehicle allows you to feel and experience the entire emotional spectrum, from joy to sadness, from love to fear.

Moving one step higher, you come to your mental body, the realm of your thoughts and ideas. This vehicle is what allows you to think, analyze, and create. It is the home of your mind.

Beyond your mind are your 3 spiritual vehicles, which make up your true essence, your purest and highest nature. They are: the manas, the buddhic body, and the atmic body. I will not go into detail about them, as that would take us away from the purpose, which is none other than to understand how these different aspects of your being influence each other.

Each of these dimensional vehicles is interconnected and corresponds to the energy centers of the Hindu tradition called chakras. They affect each other, and what happens to one of them affects the others.

The Communicating Vessels

Have you ever wondered how your emotions and thoughts affect your physical and energetic well-being? The truth is that they have a tremendous impact on your health and vitality. As the famous saying goes, *"A healthy mind in a healthy body."* This is because your thoughts and emotions are far more powerful than you can imagine.

In ancient Chinese medicine, each organ is closely associated with a specific emotion. For example, consider the relationship between the lungs and charisma. Have you noticed that when you feel full of energy, your charisma shines brighter? It's like you have a special light. Conversely, when you are overwhelmed with sadness, you feel as if your lungs are shrinking and your energy is diminishing.

But that's not all. Fear is directly related to the kidneys, while anger comes from the liver. Each emotion finds its echo in a specific organ.

Your thoughts and emotions have a direct effect on your physical health. Some emotions and thoughts make you sick, and they sap your vitality. But there are also emotions and thoughts that heal and fill you with energy and well-being.

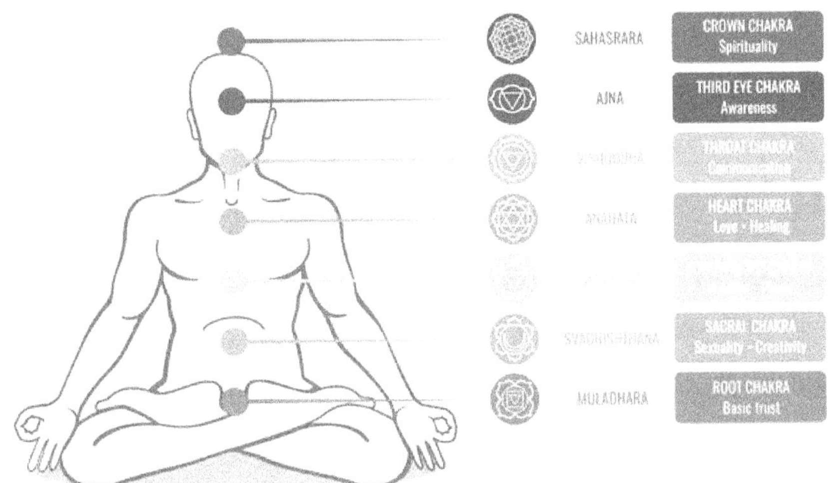

The problem arises when you become so identified with your emotions and thoughts that you lose sight of who you really are. You get caught in a loop of negativity that consumes you. Nevertheless, I want you to remember something very important: you are so much more than your fleeting emotions and thoughts. You are an infinite being of potential.

When you over-identify with your emotions and thoughts, you run the risk of losing your center of gravity, of forgetting who you really are at your core. You become more vulnerable. You stop being unbreakable and become breakable. Breakable means to break, to separate. To be breakable is to be vulnerable to being broken, to being separated.

But what happens when a vase breaks? The unity is broken, and the parts are separated. The same thing happens to you when you lose your center. The unity formed by your different dimensions—physical, mental, emotional and spiritual—becomes fragmented, and this fragmentation is at the root of many problems in all areas of your life.

You may begin to experience unexplained physical ailments, or you may feel anxious without knowing why. Perhaps your relationships are strained and conflicted, or you struggle to find meaning and purpose in your work. These are all symptoms that you have lost your connection with yourself, that you have become too identified with the ephemeral aspects of your being and have forgotten your true essence.

But here's the good news: you have the power to choose your thoughts and have control over your emotions! You are not a passive victim of them, but their creator and owner. You have the ability to take control of your mind and heart, to create inner states that nurture and strengthen you rather than weaken you.

Let's return to the analogy of tuning a radio. Your mind is like a radio with an infinite number of channels. You can choose to tune in to the station you like best at any given moment. Maybe today you feel like listening to classical music to relax, while tomorrow you will prefer something more upbeat to cheer you up. Ultimately, you choose which frequency to tune in to.

But what would happen if you lost control of the dial, suddenly you forgot you could change your tuning and found yourself stuck on a station that played only sad, melancholy songs? You'd be stuck on a frequency you didn't like, and you wouldn't know how to change it.

You will become so identified with that station that you will forget who you really are. You no longer remember that you own the radio, not vice versa. You will have given your power to something outside of you.

Imagine what it would be like to be trapped 24 hours a day, 7 days a week, on a station that plays nothing but catastrophic news and depressing songs. You can't turn it off or change it. You are doomed to listen to this endless loop of negativity. How would you feel? Undoubtably exhausted and desperate.

Well, that's precisely what happens when you over-identify with your negative thoughts and emotions. You enter a vicious cycle from which there seems to be no escape. You become obsessed with ideas that make you suffer; you relive painful situations from the past, and you anticipate future disasters that haven't happened yet.

Often, people become so identified with their thoughts and emotions that they become dominated by them. Popular literature uses phrases like "being possessed by anger" or " by fear," which happens when you allow your emotions to control you.

These emotions take over, and you become a mere passenger in your own life. You have lost your decision-making power, your ability to choose how you want to feel and what thoughts you want to have.

But remember, you are much more than your thoughts and emotions. You are the awareness that observes them. You are not the fleeting contents of your mind but the unchanging continent.

To be conscious is to be able to experience all the wonderful emotions that life has to offer, but without allowing them to possess you.

When you realize this, you regain your power. You regain control of the radio controls of your existence. You are no longer at the mercy of the random programming of your mind. Instead, you consciously choose which feel-good tune to tune into at any given moment.

The Origin of Anxiety and Somatic Therapy

Now, I would like to share a perspective that will help you understand the origin of the anxiety that is affecting you. I invite you to explore with me this vision of the human being as structured into different planes or levels of existence.

We are all like a house with many floors. You share the same foundation as everyone else, but you have your own aesthetics and decorations. Each individual, each human being, shares a basic structure with everyone else but has unique characteristics that distinguish him or her. While we all have a pair of legs, yours may be longer or stronger than someone else's. The same is true of our minds and emotions. We all have the same basic components, but how we use them and how they affect us varies from person to person.

The key to a happy and balanced life is to have all these floors of our house in harmony.

Some people are all about movement and action, like the athletes you see on TV. They like to express themselves on a physical level and their energy is focused on their bodies. Sometimes, this can lead to injury or physical problems due to over-activity.

On the other hand, there are what we might call "mental" or "emotional" people. They live inside of their heads and express themselves primarily through their minds or emotions. If they do not find a balance, they can end up with mental imbalances.

The body, mind and emotions are very much connected, so you should keep them in harmony to live better!

So, what is anxiety, and what causes it?

As I have said before, the origin of fear is emotional. Anxiety does not come from your thoughts, although it is related to them. Rather, it comes from your emotions. These are subjective interpretations of sensory data that your body sends to your brain. This data comes from every organ in your body. Modern neuroscience calls this "interoception." It's like an internal radar that alerts you when something is wrong.

Your interoception tells your brain when there is danger or a threat nearby. But here's the interesting thing: there are parts of your biology that are so primitive that they predate human language and do not respond to thought-based therapies. They are remnants of our ancestors, automatic responses that activate unexpectedly. This is why anxiety often remains, even when you use mindfulness techniques, affirmations, or other mindfulness and thought-centered practices.

Now, you might think, *but if my mind can't control these responses, what can I do?*

It's not just about changing what you think; it's about working directly with your body's signals and responses. When you experience fear, your heart beats faster, your muscles tense, and your breathing accelerates. These are automatic responses, not consciously chosen by you.

It's not that mind-based therapies don't work at all; rather, it's just that they can only affect one part of your biology.

Your mind is always trying to find a solution, but you need a more holistic approach to locate it. You can't just rely on techniques that only address the mental aspect. You have to go beyond that.

-So how can I intervene? -You insist.

The key is to help your autonomic nervous system regulate itself better. This sounds complex, but there are practical and accessible ways to do it. Somatic, body-based tools are essential for relieving accumulated stress on your nervous system. These techniques send safety signals to your brain through the proprioceptive system.

You have already learned that you can affect one level of your being by acting from another. You can influence your body from your mind and emotions, just as you can influence your thoughts and emotions from your body.

The secret is to hack your physical interoception to tell your brain that there is no danger or threat.

Remember the famous Latin phrase, *"Mens sana in corpore sano,"* which means "a healthy mind in a healthy body." It's absolutely true! If you take care of one, the other will benefit.

Somatic therapy takes advantage of this mind-body bridge that connects the physical and mental realms of human experience.

You might be wondering, *So how does this therapy work?*

It doesn't involve sitting on a therapist's couch and discussing your sensations and feelings. While this can be effective, it is not the most effective when your mind and emotions are oversaturated. Initially, the tools that will give you the most and best results will be those based on action at the most physical and energetic level. Then, when you have regained a sufficient level of peace of mind, you can also take advantage of the incredible benefits of action-based tools on the emotional and even mental levels.

So, what do I do?

The mind and body are connected, so what you experience in the mind manifests in the body. And most importantly, in your fight against anxiety, what you experience in your body manifests in your mind.

If you act with your physical body as a person without fear acts, then your mind will manifest as a person without fear.

But that sounds difficult, you say, frowning. *I'm not always in a good mood.*

To achieve this, you have to fake it first. Even if you don't feel peaceful or calm, you must pretend you do. If you do this long enough, your body's intelligence will send the message to your brain to act that way, and your brain will send the message to your mind. Remember, the brain is simply the physical seat of your mind.

So, how do I start?

Start with small gestures: an upright posture and deep, slow breathing. These physical actions send signals to your brain that all is well. It's like telling your autonomic nervous system, "I'm safe."

Gradually, these signals will resonate with your emotions and thoughts, creating a positive cycle of well-being. You don't need big changes, just small, consistent daily steps.

But don't worry, I'll show you how to put all this into practice in the next few chapters. We'll explore each technique and exercise together, and I'll ensure you understand each step. With time and dedication, you will see how these small actions will significantly change your life.

CHAPTER 3

How the Mind Works: Can We Become Addicted to Worry?

"Every form of addiction is bad, no matter whether the narcotic be alcohol, morphine or idealism."

Carl Jung

ANA HAD ALWAYS BEEN a worrier. Since childhood, she had worried about getting good grades, the opinions of others, and the well-being of her family. As she grew older, these worries consumed more and more of her time and energy.

One day, while on her way to meet her friend Laura at a coffee shop, Ana's mind began to flood with uncontrollable thoughts. "I'm going to be late for work, too," "Laura is my pity friend," "What if Laura thinks I'm a bad friend because I'm ten minutes late, and she's already gone?"

Seeing Ana's tense expression, Laura asked her what was wrong. Ana sighed and told her that she was worried about everything. Laura, who had studied psychology, explained something that would change her perspective forever.

"The human mind is incredibly complex, Ana," Laura began. "One of the fascinating aspects is how dopamine, a neurotransmitter, influences our habits and behaviors. Dopamine is released not only when we experience

something pleasurable but also when we anticipate a reward. This reward system can become addictive, even when the 'reward' is negative, such as worry."

Ana frowned, confused. "Are you saying my mind wants to worry?"

"Exactly," Laura replied. "When you worry, your brain anticipates solving those problems, which releases dopamine. Over time, your mind can become addicted to this cycle of worrying and solving, even though it causes you anxiety. It's a habit, and like all habits, it can be difficult to break."

Ana was silent, processing this new information, and after a few seconds, asked Laura, "Is there a way to change all this?"

"Yes," Laura said with a smile. "It will take time and some effort, but you can retrain your mind to break the cycle of worry. Start by recognizing when you're worrying unnecessarily, and gradually introduce new habits that help you focus on the present and the positive."

That day marked the beginning of a new chapter in Ana's life. She began to understand how her mind worked and realized that although worry had been a constant in her life, it didn't have to be her way of life. With patience and perseverance, Ana began to transform her mind and gradually overcome her anxiety.

***

When you hear the word "addiction," you probably think of physical or psychological dependence on the use of a substance or compulsive behavior that provides momentary pleasure or relief but can cause significant long-term health damage.

The truth is that addictions can manifest themselves in various ways, from dependence on substances such as alcohol, illicit drugs, or even prescription medications to compulsive behaviors related to gambling, food, sex, or the use of technology.

If you look at human behavior, you will find all kinds of addictions, some of them very subtle, such as using your cell phone all the time, overworking, and even worrying too much.

The Dopamine Reward System and Addictions

Have you ever considered the possibility that your anxiety has become a habit? Or that it is possible to become addicted to worry?

At first glance, it appears that a certain level of mental alertness helps you to perform your daily activities better. For example, when you drive a car, your state of alertness allows you to avoid danger and maneuver with caution.

However, if you dig a little deeper, you will discover that all living beings, including humans, instinctively seek pleasure and flee from pain. This basic program, engraved in the instinctual centers of all species, generates a learning system based on reward. This is known as positive and negative reinforcement.

In other words, many tend to repeat those actions that make you feel good (positive reinforcement) and avoid those that make you feel uncomfortable (negative reinforcement). This is how you unconsciously shape your habits and behaviors.

Whether it's playing a slot machine or riding a motorcycle, every day, you face situations that offer both potential risk and reward. The thrill you feel results from a complex process in your brain.

What motivates you to take these risks is the release of dopamine. This chemical doesn't just make you feel good. At first, dopamine acts like a magic bullet, captivating your brain and giving you an intense feeling of satisfaction. But if you're not careful, over time, it corrupts your internal motivation and learning mechanisms.

The dopamine reward system plays a crucial role in the feeling of pleasure you get after taking a drug or engaging in an addictive activity. This substance activates the same reward pathways in your brain that are activated when you enjoy consuming your favorite food or having sex. These pleasurable sensations are so powerful that your brain craves more and more. Thus, you become trapped in a cycle where pleasure first captures your mind; then, the dopamine reward system continues to give it to you simply by consuming something that already gives you pleasure. The result: pleasure on top of pleasure.

But there's a drawback. In this cycle, you need more and more to feel the same. What was once an exciting experience soon becomes an insatiable need. It's not that dopamine is bad. What is dangerous is the relationship that is created between its production and certain habits or routines. Dopamine itself is not to blame; it is a natural chemical and is essential for your well-being. However, you must be very careful about the actions you choose to generate this dopamine production.

In prehistoric times, reward-based learning was essential for survival. Imagine your ancestors, hungry and desperate, wandering through a hostile landscape searching for food. Suddenly, they come across a bush full of juicy berries. Their brain screams, "Calories... Survival!"

Cautiously, the hominid tastes the berries and discovers that they are delicious. Thanks to this act, he survives another day. But there's more at stake. When the caveman encountered foods rich in sugar or fat, his brain not only associated these nutrients with survival but also released dopamine. The dopamine acted as a reminder, etching in the caveman's mind: *Remember what you ate and where you found it*. Thus, he established a memory associated with the process and learned to repeat it: find food, eat, survive, and, as a dopamine bonus, feel good. It was a perfect cycle.

Today, in the developed world, finding food is not the same as the challenge our ancestors faced. Food has taken on a different role in our lives. Our modern brains have found new ways to use dopamine: "Hey, you can use this substance for more than just remembering where the food is," it seems to be telling us. And so, we've discovered that eating something delicious can make us feel better when we're feeling down.

Think about a tough day you've had in the past. Maybe you had a bad day at work, fought with your partner, or were overcome with sadness as you remembered a painful event from the past. Amid this emotional turmoil, you remembered the tempting bar of chocolate waiting for you in the fridge. That Nestlé Extra bar could be your refuge, your immediate comfort. Your brain is grateful for this brilliant idea, and you quickly learn that eating chocolate or ice cream in times of anger or sadness makes you feel better; you reward yourself with a dose of dopamine, the neurotransmitter that makes you feel good.

But now the trigger has changed: it's no longer a hunger signal coming from your stomach but an emotional signal. Feeling sad, angry, hurt, or lonely triggers your need to eat. When you do, you feel good. So, you repeat the process. And each time you do this, you reinforce this brain pathway, making it stronger and harder to break. Without realizing it, you are turning the way you deal with your emotions or try to alleviate stressful situations into a habit, or in this case, a food addiction. It's a dangerous cycle that can have serious consequences for your health.

There is also a dark side to this mechanism. The same place in the brain that processes pleasure also processes pain! It's as if your mind is trying to maintain a balance. Every time you get a jolt of pleasure, your brain generates a counter-reaction of equal intensity, producing a proportional amount of pain. In other words, the more you pursue pleasure, the more likely you are to experience negative emotions such as fear, anxiety, anger, or paranoia! It's a vicious cycle: you seek more pleasure to relieve pain, but you create more discomfort.

Because of this, you become a dopamine addict, constantly craving your next dose of satisfaction. You need more and more stimulation to get the same level of pleasure, and when you don't get it, you feel a deep sense of emptiness and frustration.

Anxiety disorders top the charts as the most common psychiatric conditions. People spend most of their time on the Internet, getting small doses of dopamine from clicking or "liking" this or that. Each of these habits and states is created by your brain.

When you enjoy something, such as a delicious piece of cake or an accomplishment at work, your brain releases dopamine, and you feel good. However, this peak of pleasure is accompanied by an inevitable crash. This crash can manifest as anxiety, distress, or even anger. It's a biological cycle designed to keep you in balance, but sometimes, it can feel like an emotional roller coaster.

It's funny how the brain works. The more you seek that intense pleasure, the more pain you can experience afterward. It's a reminder that extremes are never sustainable.

So, the key is moderation, right?

Exactly. It's not about avoiding pleasure altogether; it's about finding a healthy balance.

When you understand this biological cycle, you can begin to make more conscious decisions about how to manage the pleasure in your life. Moderation not only helps you avoid these emotional lows but also allows you to enjoy the good things in a more balanced way.

Balance is key. Find simple, everyday pleasures that don't lead to these extreme peaks and valleys. This will help you maintain a consistent and lasting sense of well-being.

Intermittent Reinforcement: Habits that Create Anxiety

You've already seen that we live in a digital age, where people spend a lot of time on the Internet and get small doses of dopamine. Let's dig a little deeper. It's not just about stress, overeating, compulsive shopping, unhealthy relationships, spending too much time online, or the general anxiety that seems to affect everyone at some point.

If you've ever been caught in a worry loop, you know exactly what I mean. In this case, a thought or emotion triggers your brain to start worrying. The result is that you avoid the negative thought or emotion, which is more rewarding than facing the original thought or emotion. It's a vicious cycle that feeds on itself. Corporations have long known this and exploited this vulnerability. The food industry invests millions of dollars to find the perfect combination of salt, sugar, and texture to make food irresistible. They trap you with flavors designed to trigger cravings and keep you eating past your satiety point.

Social networks also play with your brain. They spend countless hours perfecting their algorithms to make sure you get exactly the content that will keep you glued to your screen for hours while you consume strategically placed ads. They bombard you with carefully selected images, videos, and posts to trigger your reward centers and keep you hooked.

The media is not far behind. They optimize their headlines to attract clicks by appealing to your emotions and curiosity. They tempt you with sensational stories and addictive content to keep you consuming more and more.

Even online retailers use psychological tricks. They design their websites with enticements like "other customers like you have bought..." to keep you browsing and adding items to your cart until you finally make a purchase, often of things you don't really need.

These tactics are everywhere and are getting more sophisticated and intense every day. But what's worse is that there are other, even more powerful "addiction maximizers." One of them is intermittent reinforcement, the most fear-inducing type of reward learning. When you receive a reward in a casual or seemingly random way, the dopaminergic neurons in your brain are activated more than ever. The uncertainty of not knowing when the next reward will come keeps you hooked, craving the thrill repeatedly.

Remember that special occasion when someone surprised you with an unexpected gift or surprise party? Sure you do; that moment is etched in your memory, right? That's because unexpected rewards trigger dopamine in your brain at a much higher rate than expected.

Casinos are experts at taking advantage of this mechanism. They have perfected intermittent reinforcement to the point where they have a secret formula that makes slot machines "hit" just enough times to keep you playing, even though almost everyone loses money in the long run. That's the casino's "winning" formula.

However, intermittent reinforcement is not limited to casinos. It's present in anything that alerts you to something new. Your email, Facebook, Instagram, WhatsApp, that shelf search at Leroy Merlin... They all exploit addiction to the fullest precisely because their notifications don't come at regular intervals.

The second great addiction-enhancer in the modern world is instant availability. In the 19th century, significant effort was required to buy new shoes. Back then, if you wanted a pair of shoes for your kids, you couldn't buy them impulsively, knowing they'd be at your house the next day with Amazon Prime. The process was tedious, time-consuming, and far from instantaneous, forcing you to carefully weigh the costs and benefits. Were your old boots really worn out, or could they last a little longer? This extra time was crucial to allow the initial excitement to subside and give way to a more thoughtful analysis of your needs.

But in the modern world, you can satisfy almost any need or desire almost instantly. Stressed out? No problem, there's a bakery around the corner. Bored? Check out the latest videos on YouTube. Need a new pair of shoes because you saw someone wearing a pair you liked? Log on to Amazon, and they'll be on their way to your house in a few clicks.

Here's the kicker. By combining the reward-based learning of your instinctive brain with intermittent reinforcement and instant availability, you have a disastrous recipe for modern habits and addictions. I'm not telling you this to scare you but because I want you to understand how your mind works and how much of today's world is designed to create and profit from addictive behaviors.

But don't be discouraged, for there is good news. To use your mind successfully, you must first understand how it works, which is what you are doing right now by reading this chapter. Once you understand the mechanics of your mind, you can begin to work with it instead of fighting its natural tendencies.

It's that simple. Now you know how your mind creates habits. And with that knowledge, you're ready to take the next step: identifying habits and creating new ones.

Anxiety as a Habit Loop

Anxiety and stress can become a habit loop, like a trap that closes in on you without you even realizing it. To understand why this happens, we need to look at your brain.

Your mind doesn't like uncertainty. On the contrary, it wants to have everything under control and put into clear categories to feel safe. When you are faced with uncertain situations, whether your life is in danger from a wild animal attack or you have to give a speech in front of an audience without knowing if you will do it well, your mind and brain react the same way: with discomfort, anxiety, worry, and nervous tension.

The stress or anxiety then becomes the trigger that drives you to seek a solution to the problem, which temporarily reduces the anxiety. You may not always find the perfect solution, but if you succeed enough times, a cycle of repetition is perpetuated. It's like going to the casino and playing a slot machine. If you win a few times, you feel the urge to play again and again. Your mind is similarly conditioned.

Numerous research studies have shown that anxiety perpetuates itself as a loop of negatively reinforced habits. Your brain, in its eagerness to help you survive, once associated problem-solving with worrying. As a result, it now thinks that worrying is the best way to deal with difficulties.

Worry works as a mental behavior that makes you feel like you have some control because, in theory, you are trying to solve a problem. But the reality is that the worry itself becomes the problem.

When these worry processes are repeated at certain intervals, you create ingrained habits. Habits are nothing more than repeated processes that create specific neural connections in your brain and in your sympathetic and parasympathetic systems that determine your daily behavior. That's why it's so important to understand how a habit is formed. You need to understand the mechanisms behind the creation of thought and behavior patterns so you can take control of them and transform them into something positive for your life. In the next chapter, I will show you in detail how habits are formed and the practical steps you can take to start changing them. See you soon!

CHAPTER 4

Neurochemical Basis of Habit Formation

"People do not decide their futures; they decide their habits, and their habits decide their futures."

Frederick Matthias Alexander

ESTHER, A YOUNG 24-YEAR-OLD *singer, finds herself, one more day, in the rehearsal studio, practicing tirelessly for her big chance: to make it to the finals of Got Talent. With her guitar in hand and her voice as her only weapon, Esther is determined to reach the pinnacle of success.*

The studio walls are covered with concert posters and photographs of successful artists. The dim lighting creates a warm, intimate atmosphere, ideal for cultivating an environment where Esther can concentrate.

She stands in front of the microphone, adjusts her guitar, and begins to sing the first notes of her song. However, something goes wrong. Her voice cracks unexpectedly, and she stops dead in her tracks. She pauses and reflects for a moment. She takes a deep breath and tries again, this time at a much slower pace. Each time she misses a note, she stops, adjusts her posture and returns to the beginning or to the exact spot where she missed.

She sings and stops, and again, sings and stops, again and again, without rest. Her determination is unwavering. She knows that each attempt brings her closer to her goal. Every off-key note is an opportunity to improve. She takes a deep breath, centers herself and starts again.

And then, suddenly, everything falls into place. On the seventh time, Esther, without making a single mistake, sings the entire song with absolute perfection. Her voice flows with clarity and emotion that she has never felt before.

At that moment, Esther knows she is one step closer to her dream. The Got Talent final no longer seems so far away. With her guitar in hand and her voice steady, Esther is ready to conquer the stage and make her dream come true.

***

Daniel Coyle, in his book *The Talent Code* (2009), explains the fascinating neurochemical basis that leads to automating learning and creating new habits.

For you to get the most out of everything that follows, it is important to remember that a habit is nothing more than a process repeated to the point where it becomes automatic.

Every human skill, whether it's a new dance step, riding a bike, or establishing a new habit in your life, is based on creating new neural connections. These connections are chains of nerve fibers that carry tiny electrical impulses. In simple terms, it is a signal that travels through a circuit.

Each time you practice what you're learning, the brain secretes a substance called myelin, which strengthens and reinforces the neural circuits being activated. Myelin is the holy grail of learning and creating new habits. From Michelangelo's masterful brushstrokes to Michael Jordan's spectacular leaps, all creative people have depended on this substance. The best part is that you're not born with a set amount of myelin—it can grow over time. Like anything that grows, it can be developed and strengthened with practice.

Myelin's key role is to wrap around nerve fibers, much like rubber insulation around a copper wire. This helps make signals in your brain stronger and faster by keeping electrical impulses from leaking out. Each time you practice something—like a martial arts move or a guitar note—myelin adds more layers of insulation around the neural circuits you're using. With each new layer, your skills become a bit faster and more precise.

The thicker the myelin, the better it insulates the circuits, and the faster and more precise your movements and thoughts become until you reach the point where they become automated, and you no longer need to consciously think about them.

In other words, **practice and repetition** make the myelin-covered neural circuits fire much faster. Think of it as building a neural highway, where each repetition adds a new layer of pavement, making the ride smoother and faster each time.

So, when you're faced with the task of developing a new skill or habit, remember that every repetition counts. You're building those neural circuits bit by bit, layer by layer, until they become something that works automatically for you.

The secretion of myelin explains the two key phases of learning and creating new habits.

The first is *conscious learning*, where deliberate effort is required to create new neural connections. It's like when you first learn to drive; every gear change and use of the clutch demands your full attention.

With constant practice, you move into the second phase: *subconscious learning*. Here, myelin has strengthened and isolated those neural circuits, allowing them to activate automatically. This is why an experienced driver can shift gears without even thinking about it.

This is the physiological basis that explains why practice and repetition are the key to learning any skill and establishing a new habit in your life. It's a truism we often forget, but science reminds us again and again. Even so-called "natural talent" is nothing without constant practice.

Malcolm Gladwell, in his book *Outliers* (2008), quantifies an expert's talent at a minimum of 10,000 hours of practice. He uses this to explain the genius of Mozart, the Beatles, Bruce Lee, and many others.

So, remember that every time you repeat an action or gesture, you are strengthening those neural circuits, wrapping them with another layer of myelin, making them faster and more efficient. The more you do it, the more automatic it'll become until you no longer have to pay your conscious attention.

Now you understand how these unhealthy habits have taken hold in your life, don't you? Without realizing it, you have been constantly repeating certain actions, creating neural circuits that reinforce those behaviors.

This is not something new that modern science has discovered. In fact, it corroborates the ancient Hermetic knowledge of the principle of rhythm. The sages and philosophers of old understood this process.

When you repeatedly think or act, you form a mental pattern that feels alive. It's as if you're nurturing an independent idea in your mind. The more you engage in a habit or belief, the stronger and more autonomous it becomes. Eventually, these habits or beliefs can feel so ingrained that they seem to operate on their own, no longer requiring your conscious choice.

The worst thing is that sometimes those habits and limiting beliefs acquire so much strength that you are the one who depends on them, especially if your will is weak. You become a slave to your own neural creations, to your thought patterns, trapped in a vicious cycle from which there seems to be no escape. Your fears and anxieties take over, dictating your decisions and actions.

Modern science explains and attributes it to chemical changes in the brain, but the ancients already intuited this process and expressed it in more symbolic and spiritual terms. In the end, both perspectives point to the same fundamental truth: what you focus your energy on constantly ends up manifesting in your reality, for better or worse. That is why it is crucial to choose your neural creations appropriately; once created, they possess their own entity and great power.

***

As I have already explained, your mind and brain are designed to seek pleasure. Therefore, the vast majority of your behavioral habits have been formed based on that search, whether through food, drink, sex, or any other activity that generates satisfaction. But this is not always the case. Let's delve a little deeper into the ancient hermetic principle of rhythm.

According to this universal principle, if you repeat something rhythmically for long enough, even if it is not pleasurable or even if it's painful, the result will be the same: a brain circuit will be created that will be reflected in your life as an ingrained habit of your personality.

Think about it for a moment. When you have recurring, obsessive thoughts, when you find yourself caught in cycles of stress or anxiety, the process is identical. In other words, every time you repeat those thoughts, you strengthen those neural circuits, wrapping them with more and more myelin and increasing their bioelectrical conductivity and power over you.

During episodes of anxiety, several brain circuits are created simultaneously in your brain. One of them relates to the desperate search for relief from the tension created by the difficult situation you are facing. This circuit produces dopamine and is, therefore, pleasurable. At the same time, there is the brain circuit that generates tension and is a precursor to the circuit that generates feelings of relief or pleasure. This means that your mind creates an association between stress and the gratification you feel when you finally get rid of it. This will inevitably generate a habit in which the stress is linked with the pleasure of its release, an endless cycle that is difficult to escape from.

Yes, although it may seem strange at first, the process of addiction formation is exactly the same. That is why you must understand that habits related to overthinking, obsession, anxiety, and stress are, in fact, addictions of your mind. I emphasize 'of your mind' because brain circuits are always a reflection of your mind's behavior.

As an ancient Chinese proverb says: *"Bad habits come as passengers, visit us as guests and stay as masters."* We become slaves to our habits, and bad habits can have a devastating effect on our lives. You must identify these unhealthy habits and consciously replace them with more beneficial ones.

I want you to understand the importance of being selective and careful about the actions you take in your life. You have already understood that the repetition of these negative actions will create brain connections that will be incorporated into your subconscious and automatic behavior. Every thought, every emotion and every act you repeat is molding your brain and, therefore, your reality.

You are like a sculptor shaping his or her masterpiece with each chisel stroke. Each blow of the hammer is an action you perform, and the final sculpture is the result of all those accumulated blows. What kind of masterpiece do you want to create: one that is a reflection of unhealthy and limiting habits or one that embodies the best version of yourself?

You have the power to choose which actions to repeat and, therefore, which habits to install in your life. It is an immense responsibility but also an incredible opportunity. You can deliberately design your mind and your life through the actions you choose to take.

So be conscious and be intentional. Choose thoughts, emotions and actions that are aligned with the person you want to be and the life you want to live. Remember, every repetition counts; every action matters. You are sculpting your mind and your reality with every choice you make.

The two key elements that will allow you to create and institute new healthy habits, as well as improve your performance in any area of your life, are:

1. **Conscious practice or repetition**. You've probably heard countless times that practice is the key to success, and it's true. But what you may not know is that certain types of practice can boost your skills up to ten times faster than conventional practice.

It's not just about practicing for the sake of practice but doing it intentionally, challenging yourself, correcting your mistakes and constantly seeking improvement. Only then will you be able to accelerate your learning and reach levels of mastery that seemed unattainable before.

2. **Passionate motivation**. We all need a little motivation to start any project or undertake any change in our lives. But what really sets true achievers apart from the rest is a much higher level of commitment, an overwhelming passion that stems from their deepest desires.

When you find that spark that ignites your inner fire, when you connect with your purpose and your truest goals, motivation ceases to be an effort and becomes a natural drive that pushes you forward, even in the most difficult moments.

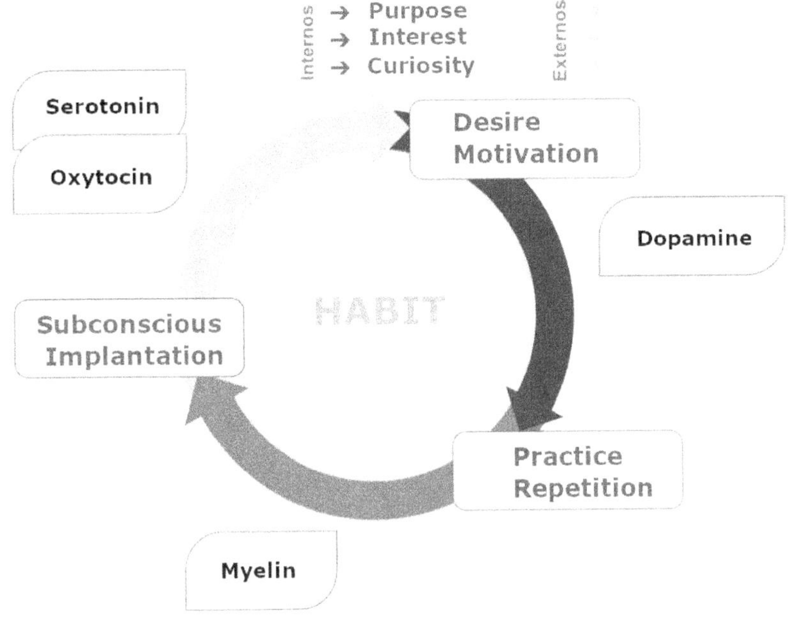

The Power of Habits

Motivation is the spark that will start the virtuous circle of creating new habits and routines that will transform your existence. But where does that motivation come from? How can you activate it and keep it alive?

The answer lies in your emotions. Remember that, as a multidimensional human being, your emotions are the master key that opens the doors of creation. In every creative process, there is a masculine element that fertilizes and a feminine element that receives and gestates. In this case, it is your emotions that fertilize your thoughts, giving birth to new brain circuits according to the actions you undertake.

But be careful; do not let yourself be seduced by ephemeral external factors such as novelty or surprise. While they may be useful in arousing your initial interest, they are difficult to sustain over time. You can't depend on something continuing to strike you as novel every day to keep you motivated.

Instead, the real secret lies in finding a firm purpose, a goal that resonates with the deepest part of you. That purpose will become the best motivating factor you can have. External stimuli can serve as triggers to inspire that excitement, but it will be your internal connection to that goal that fuels your long-term motivation.

And this is where the magical power of habits comes into play. When you repeat an action long enough, the myelin that coats your neural circuits causes that action to become increasingly automatic, requiring less willpower to initiate it. In other words, habit puts your motivation on autopilot. You no longer need to question the why of your actions. You simply execute them naturally and fluidly.

So, if you can make something motivate you enough to make it a habit through constant practice, you will have found the path to mastery in any area of your life.

First, the Work, Then the Pleasure

Let me tell you a fascinating story that illustrates the addictive power of our old friend, dopamine. In a scientific experiment, a lever was placed in a mouse cage. Each time the mouse operated the lever, it received a small jolt of dopamine. As expected, the mouse became addicted to pressing the lever.

But the surprising thing was that the mouse eventually died of starvation because it stopped eating! Compared to the euphoria of pressing the lever, the desire to eat did not generate enough dopamine to motivate the rodent to break away from the lever and forage for food.

Now, think about how this example relates to your own life. Anxious situations lead you to look for apparent solutions that generate huge amounts of dopamine in your brain. This is what makes things such as scrolling through social media and binge-watching TV so addictive.

Other activities, such as exercising or feeling the satisfaction of accomplishment, pale in comparison to the dopamine-generating capacity of these "false solutions" to anxiety. As in the mouse experiment, the greatest danger of addictions is what they make you stop doing. This is why developing the capacity for self-control and, in particular, the ability to postpone immediate gratifications is critical. Your goal should be to associate the release of dopamine with the establishment of conscious, healthy habits.

In other words, make adopting the healthy habits you will learn in the next chapters a motivating factor so that your brain interprets dopamine as a reward for doing your "shoulds."

It's not about eliminating dopamine; it's about changing the source from which it comes.

Going for a walk outdoors or practicing yoga, for example, not only improves your physical condition but will also increase your dopamine levels sustainably.

Another healthy source of dopamine is eating a balanced diet. Getting a good night's sleep also plays an important role; good rest allows your brain to naturally regulate its dopamine levels.

However, on the flip side of the coin, when you generate a relationship between your dopamine production and unhealthy habits, then you have a problem.

It's a matter of choosing wisely. Dopamine is a key neurotransmitter in the process of reinforcing behaviors. Every time you experience pleasure, whether it's eating your favorite food, listening to a song you love, or receiving praise, your brain releases a dose of dopamine. This chemical makes you feel good and motivates you to repeat the action that gave you that pleasant feeling.

Becoming aware of this mechanism is the first step in breaking the cycle. Remember, you have the power to shape your reality. Every thought, every action, and every choice counts. Choose wisely and build a life that truly fills you with happiness from within.

Think of activities that bring you joy without causing an extreme reaction in your brain: reading a good book, spending time with friends or practicing a creative hobby. These small doses of happiness contribute to a more stable state of mind and remove you from the harmful pleasure-pain cycle.

Always remember, you are in control. You just need to make the right choices. In the following chapters, you will learn about them.

If you get motivated and passionate about the idea of transforming your life through the tools this book offers you, you will never again have to suffer from your mental processes. Imagine what your life will be like when you have established healthy and conscious habits. Let that vision inspire you and propel you into action.

Always remember: *"Work first, then pleasure."* Or better yet: *"Work first, then reward."* You must learn to postpone immediate gratifications and prioritize actions that will lead you to your long-term goals, i.e., long-term gratifications. Like the mouse in the experiment, if you get carried away by instant gratification, you could lose sight of what really matters.

If the mouse had learned to press the lever only after eating, perhaps it would still be alive and happy, enjoying both the food and the dopamine rush as a reward for its discipline. Always remember to apply this principle to your own life: do what you must do first, and then enjoy the satisfaction of having achieved it.

In the following chapters, you will learn tools that, if practiced with consistency and motivation, will allow you, in time, to be rewarded with enough dopamine to be happy.

Train your brain to associate dopamine with the establishment of positive habits. Each time you complete one of the tasks or exercises in this book, take a moment to savor the feeling of accomplishment. Celebrate each small step you take toward your transformation. Over time, your mind will crave that dopamine reward that comes from doing the right thing for yourself.

CHAPTER 5
Physical-Pranic Level

"If you want to find the secrets of the universe, think in terms of energy, frequency and vibration."

Nicola Tesla

In the not-too-distant future, technology will transform the environment. Buildings will come alive with facades that adapt to the weather and your preferences. Sidewalks will light up as you pass, guiding you to your destination. Traffic lights synchronize with traffic flow, optimizing every second of your journey.

In this city of smart gadgets, every object you encounter will seem to have a specific purpose. Trash garbage cans will open automatically as you approach, sorting waste for easy recycling. Streetlights will turn on and off as needed, saving energy without compromising your safety. Even the park benches will adjust to your posture, giving you maximum comfort.

At dawn, the alarm clock breaks the silence with its beeping. Its call awakens not only you but also the coffee pot in the kitchen, which begins to bubble and whistle, preparing a cup of coffee that floods the house with its aroma, inviting you to get up and face the day. As you sit up, the blinds open gently, allowing the sunlight to caress your face and help you fully awaken. It's as if the whole house is conspiring to ensure you start your day on the right foot.

Once you've had breakfast and left the dwelling on your way to work, the city of smart gadgets continues its day as if it has a life of its own. A silent but efficient dance takes place in your absence, keeping your home in tip-top shape.

The robotic vacuum cleaner begins its daily run in the living room with almost human determination. It glides with fluid movements, zigzagging among the furniture with a clear purpose: to leave every nook and cranny spotless.

The refrigerator, too, seems to be awake, like a silent guardian of your nutrition. Its shelves are full of perfectly organized foods, ready to help you make healthy choices when you return home.

In another corner of the house, the computer and printer work tirelessly, the rollers spinning and spitting out sheets of paper with printed text and graphics.

At 6:30 p.m., the kitchen robot begins its work. With precision and efficiency, the device weighs ingredients, cuts vegetables and adjusts temperatures, all programmed so that your dinner is ready just in time.

When you return home at 7:00 p.m., the atmosphere around you comes alive. Automatically, the television turns on its screen, filling the room with the buzz of the news and programs of the moment.

You sit down at the table, where a plate of tasty Rioja-style lentils prepared with care by the food processor awaits you.

You observe with satisfaction how all these appliances work in perfect harmony, connected by an invisible network of energy: the electricity that flows through each cable and plug, feeding each device and giving them that apparent life they possess. It's as if your home were a living organism, breathing and moving to the rhythm of your needs and desires.

One day, however, something unexpected happens.

A storm rages over the city. Suddenly, the power goes out without warning, plunging your home into an eerie silence. In a moment, all those appliances that were once brimming with life and activity become inert, as if they had lost their soul.

Your alarm clock stops its constant beeping. The coffee maker, while brewing your daily dose of caffeine, stops abruptly. The robotic vacuum cleaner, once so diligent, stands motionless in the middle of the living room.

The refrigerator, the guardian of your food, stops cooling. The television, your window to the outside world, shuts off. Your computer, the center of your work and entertainment, goes silent. The printer, caught in the middle of its task, leaves a sheet half-printed as if time had frozen at that precise moment.

The city, once a hustle and bustle of activity, is plunged into a profound silence. The devices, which seemed to have a life of their own, are now mere objects without purpose. Everything that gave them life had disappeared with the electricity. During the storm, the City of Intelligent Devices was plunged into darkness.

When electricity was finally restored, the devices came back to life, continuing their tasks as if nothing had happened.

Although these devices seemed to have a life of their own, their existence depended entirely on the energy that powered them.

***

This story invites us to reflect on our own lives. What is that invisible energy that drives us? What would happen if, suddenly, that life force were to disappear?

Prana is to yoga what electricity is to our civilization. This analogy is no exaggeration; *prana*, that vital energy that permeates the entire universe, is as essential to your well-being as electricity is to the functioning of our cities.

So what is *prana*? Imagine *prana* as the spark of life flowing through you. This concept comes from ancient Indian spiritual and philosophical traditions. It is not just an abstract idea; it is a tangible force that affects your body, mind and spirit.

When you are stressed, your *prana* levels are low or unbalanced. That lack of vital energy can make you feel restless and exhausted. When you learn to balance and increase your *prana* levels, you cultivate a sense of calm, clarity and well-being.

According to yoga, *prana* is the source and sum total of all the universe's energies, and you are an integral part of this cosmic flow. There is a profound relationship between the universe (macrocosm) and you as a human being (microcosm). *Prana* is also the energy that animates you, its most tangible manifestation being your breath.

But *prana* is not only present in the air. It is also present in the food you eat, the water you drink, and the sunlight that bathes your skin.

Prana is something that exists outside of you and flows within your being, nourishing every cell of your body and every thought of your mind.

Prana permeates your whole body, even where air cannot reach. It is your true nourishment because, without it, no life is possible.

Yoga practitioners proclaim that *prana* can be stored and accumulated in the nervous system, more specifically in the solar plexus. They also stress this fundamental and crucial idea: that this flow of *prana* can be controlled at will through thought.

You can learn to channel *prana* to improve all aspects of your life with practice and dedication. It is as if you suddenly have access to a switch that controls your vitality and overall well-being.

The most important source of *prana* is the atmosphere, and you can tap into it. Long before science discovered electricity, yogis had already perceived something amazing: the atmosphere vibrates with a subtle energy that is the main source of all energies acting in the human body. It is as if the air you breathe were charged with an invisible but powerful life force.

This idea does not contradict modern Western theories but complements them. When you compare the ancient yogic and Taoist traditions with the modern observations and discoveries of Western science, you come to a fascinating conclusion: the *prana* in the atmosphere is made up, if not entirely, at least to a large extent, of electrical particles, such as negative ions.

One of the least understood aspects of the Taoist tradition is the importance of *yin-yang*.

Yin and *yang* are not opposing forces but are complementary; they are in constant flux and transformation.

The Chinese attribute the origin of positive yang energy to the Sun and the stars, while attributing the origin of negative yin energy to the Earth. Imagine these forces as two invisible currents constantly flowing around you. Yang represents light and the essence of purity. It is the energy that rises above, forming the sky. Yin, on the other hand, is dense and heavy, embodying what has taken shape and solidified to create the Earth. While the energy of the sky remains above, it nourishes plants and vegetation below.

Have you ever wondered how the ancient Chinese were able to perceive these subtle forces more than 4,000 years ago? How did they manage to distinguish, under the name of yang energy, the positive atmospheric electricity and, as yin energy, the negative charge of the Earth?

On the other hand, you should know that a real metabolism exists in your body of the electricity you take in from the surrounding air. You are a living battery, constantly recharging yourself with energy from the environment.

Every time you breathe deeply, especially in nature, you absorb this vital force that revitalizes and balances you.

The issue goes much deeper than you might imagine, focusing on the ionization of the atmosphere and its profound impact on human bioelectrical metabolism and, thus, on your health.

You have likely witnessed powerful electrical discharges in the form of lightning during a thunderstorm; they are a spectacular manifestation of this ionization, discharging a jaw-dropping amount of energy. But what you may not know is that atmospheric electricity is a constant presence all around you, even when the sky is clear. It is always there, subtly influencing your body, even if you can't always see or feel it directly. This invisible reality affects you more than you might think, and understanding how it works is key to improving your well-being.

An ion is an atom or molecule that has gained or lost one or more electrons, acquiring an electrical charge, and you may be surprised to learn how essential they are to your cellular life.

There are two main types of ions: negative ions and positive ions.

When you inhale negative ions, atoms or molecules negatively charged because they have acquired extra electrons, your body benefits greatly. These ions are abundant in the atmosphere and in natural environments such as forests, coastlines, mountain ranges and near waterfalls.

In urban environments, you are surrounded by atoms and molecules that, by shedding some of their electrons, acquire a positive electrical charge, thus becoming positive ions. These ions are largely the product of environmental pollution, the electronic devices you use every day and various materials used in the construction of buildings and homes around you.

By inhaling negative ions, you counteract the effect of positive ions, which helps balance serotonin in your brain. This neurotransmitter plays a key role in controlling your mood and anxiety levels.

By coming into contact with negative ions, you will also experience a decrease in the levels of cortisol circulating in your body, the hormone associated with stress and anxiety. As a result, you will notice how a pleasant feeling of peace and tranquility invades you, allowing you to reach a deeper state of relaxation and considerably reducing the tension accumulated in your nerves. This means that when you walk through the countryside, you notice a significant difference in how you feel. The air seems fresher and cleaner, and you feel more energized. It's not just your imagination; it's a direct result of a higher concentration of beneficial negative ions.

In the city, however, you may experience a feeling of heaviness or fatigue that you can't explain. This is a direct consequence of the reduced presence of these vital ions in the urban environment.

All this scientific knowledge is in line with ancient Eastern traditions: *prana*, that essential life force, is not just a specific chemical component of the air you breathe. It is much more than that.

Negative ionization of oxygen atoms involves adding electrical energy to them, which only occurs under the influence of important sources of energy that are all around you. Among these sources are natural emanations from the ground, such as gamma rays from certain rocks that subtly ionize the air you breathe.

The sun is the main source of vitalizing negative ions because of its short-wave radiation.

Cosmic rays radiate you endlessly, day and night, passing through clouds and soil.

Have you ever noticed that you feel more energy after a day at the beach? It's because moving or evaporating masses of water produce life-giving ions, making the coastal air very revitalizing. On the coast, you are immersed in an ocean of *prana*, sometimes even too intense for ultra-sensitive organisms.

Let's now take a look at how electricity metabolism works in animals, including humans. This fascinating process involves the absorption of tiny negative ions to electrically charge the organism, eliminating excess electricity through the skin.

The body is a living battery: the electrical reserves need to be charged to the maximum and the skin must be allowed to evacuate the surplus to maintain an optimal balance.

Mammals, unlike cold-blooded animals such as lizards, have a constant electrical exchange with the atmosphere due to the regulation of their body temperature.

The loss and absorption of negative ions is a continuous and necessary process, similar to respiration. This is why sunbathing (yang) is incredibly beneficial for you, and your body must remain connected to the earth (yin) to allow for a constant electrical discharge.

When you walk barefoot in the grass or lie on the sand at the beach, you are facilitating this vital electrical exchange. It's one of the reasons you feel so refreshed after spending time in nature.

All animals are subject to this *"permanent electrotherapy."* Fur acts as a thermal insulator and facilitates the evacuation of electricity. The paws ensure direct contact with the ground, and, in turn, their "grounding."

In your case, as a modern human being, the clothes and shoes you wear every day act as electrical insulators, reducing your natural vitality by preventing the normal evacuation of electricity from your body. You may not realize it, but this artificial barrier between your skin and the earth has a significant impact on your well-being.

People who wear little or no clothing maintain greater vitality and connection to their environment. However, when these groups adopt Western clothing, their vital energy decreases significantly. This phenomenon is a direct consequence of losing electrical contact with the earth.

I invite you to reflect on how you might incorporate more moments of direct connection with nature into your daily life. Even small gestures, such as walking barefoot on the grass or sitting on the ground for a few minutes, can help you restore that electrical balance so necessary for your vitality.

Sauna, Sport and *Prana*

Be mindful, because once you understand the mechanism, you will realize that a living being that is negatively charged by absorbing negative ions through breathing can also do so by emitting positive ions through the evaporation of water. And if there is one place where you are subjected to abundant evaporation, it is certainly during a sauna session or when you do sports and sweat.

Think about how you feel after a sauna session: light, refreshed, full of energy. It's as if you have recharged your internal batteries. This feeling of well-being is not only physical but also mental and emotional. Right? This effect cannot be attributed solely to the elimination of toxins. The opening of the capillaries and the activation of blood circulation throughout your entire body produce a general toning that can largely explain these sauna effects. However, that feeling of "dynamism," that feeling of being "charged," comes from an increase in the electrical charge of your body.

You possess an energetic body that gives you life. The difference between a living body and a corpse is essentially that one possesses *prana* and the other does not.

And you have already seen that one of the largest *prana* reservoirs is in the air. Have you ever stopped to think about why it is so necessary for a newborn baby to take its first breath? According to certain teachings, it is just at the moment of that first inhalation that the spiritual essence penetrates you; that is when you really incarnate into a living being.

And what happens when a person passes away? Have you ever wondered why, when someone dies, they are said to have expired?

Funny, inhale at birth, expire at death! These patterns are not casual but respond to a profound meaning that I cannot expand on here for obvious reasons.

Following Swami Sivananda's wise adage, *"An ounce of practice is worth more than tons of theory,"* all these theoretical considerations you are learning will soon have practical applications in your daily life.

So get ready, in the next few chapters, to discover how you can incorporate this knowledge into your daily routine and experience firsthand the benefits of this wonderful life energy that surrounds you.

CHAPTER 6
Pretending Isn't So Bad

"Act the way you'd like to be, and soon you'll be the way you act."

Bob Dylan

AGUSTIN WAS A GOOD-NATURED, kind and considerate man, but he had always been withdrawn and somewhat shy. He worked as a librarian in a small town, where he spent his days among books and silence. Although his colleagues and friends liked him, they noticed his lack of confidence and encouraged him to participate more in social activities. However, Agustin always found excuses to avoid any situation that would take him out of his comfort zone.

One day, his best friend, Julio, convinced him to accompany him to a meeting of the neighborhood parish group. The parish was organizing various community activities, and they had recently decided to stage a play called "Don Armando Gresca," written by Adrian Ortega. They needed actors, and Julio thought it would be a good opportunity for Agustin to come out of his shell. Reluctantly, Agustin agreed to go, more to please his friend than out of real interest.

As he watched others participate at the parish, something inside him awakened. Seeing the passion and energy of the amateur actors, he felt a spark of curiosity. When they mentioned that they still needed someone for the lead role of Don Armando, a charismatic, bold and full-of-life man, Julio did not hesitate to propose Agustin. Surprised and unable to refuse, Agustín found himself accepting the challenge.

The first rehearsals were difficult. Agustin felt ridiculous trying to adopt the confidence and gallantry of Don Armando Gresca Segura. But little by little, under the director's patient guidance and the parish group's support, he began to get into character. Soon, not only did he recite the lines with confidence, but his posture, voice and demeanor reflected the essence of Don Armando.

Six months later, on opening day, Agustin completely transformed himself into Don Armando Gresca on stage. The audience was delighted with his performance and gave him a standing ovation at the end of the play. But the real transformation occurred offstage.

In his daily life, Agustin began to notice changes in his personality. He no longer felt uncomfortable speaking in public; his voice was firmer, and his presence more confident. At social gatherings, he took the initiative in conversations, and his colleagues in the library were surprised to see him making decisions with unusual confidence.

One day, while walking in the park, Agustin ran into Julio.

"You look different," his friend commented. "What happened?"

Agustin smiled. "I've been playing Don Armando Gresca for six months. I think something of him has stayed with me."

Julio laughed. "See, I knew theater was your thing."

From then on, Agustin continued to participate in plays with more enthusiasm and confidence each time. His life became filled with new experiences and friendships, and although he never ceased to be the kind and considerate man he had always been, he now also carried with him the boldness and charisma of Don Armando Gresca.

***

When you change your posture and body language, you also change your mind. I know this may sound like a joke, but it's totally true. When you feel sad and depressed, you tend to look down at the ground with your shoulders slumped and adopt the typical posture of someone dejected. Of course you do.

Now, I suggest you try something different: stand up straight, stick out your chest, lift your shoulders and keep your head up; you can even exaggerate it a bit by looking up. Do it right now and see how you feel. Do you notice any difference? I'm sure you do. Your mood instantly changes as you adopt a more upright and open posture.

Don't underestimate the power your body has over your mind. Use this simple postural trick every time you feel down and see for yourself how your energy and outlook transform in a matter of seconds. Your body is a powerful tool to transform your thoughts and emotions; use it to your advantage!

No one can feel sad when they are laughing. Try it. Even if you don't feel like laughing, make a conscious effort to smile. Feel the muscles in your face tighten and the corners of your mouth lift. Let that smile expand into a laugh, even if it is forced at first.

Sure, you'll tell me, *but I don't feel like laughing*. And it's true. Maybe at this moment you don't feel like it at all. But that's where your willingness to act as if you feel like laughing comes into play. You have the power to choose your attitude and your emotional response to any situation.

Don't worry if it's hard at first. It's normal to feel a little weird or unnatural forcing a laugh when you're not in the mood for it. Just fake it until you make it. With practice, you'll be amazed at how that fake laugh transforms into a genuine, contagious laugh. Your mood will improve dramatically, and you'll see things from a more positive perspective. Try it and see the power of laughter for yourself.

Act as if you have already achieved your goal. Energetic channels will open that will put you in touch with that vibration or emotion you wish to manifest. It is a cosmic law that modern neuroscience is recently beginning to rediscover. You send a powerful signal to the universe when you act as if you have already achieved your goal. You align your thoughts, feelings and actions with the reality you want to create. And by doing so for long enough, that reality will have no choice but to manifest in your life.

Act as if you already have the calmness and peace of mind you desire. Speak with a soft but firm tone of voice like a confident and calm person. Walk upright like someone who is at peace with himself and the world with purposeful but unhurried steps. Maintain a relaxed but confident body posture, with your shoulders back and your head held high, reflecting the inner security you already possess. Smile serenely, knowing that all is well.

The more you act like the calm, confident person you want to be, the faster it will become your reality!

Your subconscious can't tell the difference between reality and imagination. Use this to your advantage by acting as if you already have something you want to have: a strength or a quality.

One study has shown that if you hold "power poses" for as little as 2 minutes, you get a 20% increase in your testosterone levels, which improves your self-confidence. At the same time, this simple practice reduces your cortisol levels by 25%, helping to reduce stress and anxiety.

Adopting these expansive body postures, such as standing with your hands on your hips, sitting with your legs apart or extending your arms in victory, sends signals to your brain that you are powerful, capable and in control. Incorporate these "power" exercises into your daily routine, and you'll notice how your mind and body synchronize to a state of greater security and serenity.

Tool: Pretend, Act as If

Like Agustín when he started doing theater, I invite you to spend about five minutes each day in front of a mirror, moving and acting as a calm, peaceful person would. Pay close attention to your reflection and observe each gesture and movement. Repeatedly correct any gestures that need adjustment. Allow your movements to be slow and deliberate, accompanied by deep, steady breathing. Don't forget to smile genuinely, letting your expression radiate inner serenity.

Throughout the day, when you feel yourself rushing or notice anxiety or stress starting to take hold, return to this calmer, more grounded persona. Take a deep breath and slow down, just as you did in front of the mirror. At first, you may only be able to maintain this calm for a few minutes, but this new persona will grow stronger with consistent practice and perseverance. With enough dedication, it will gradually replace the old version of you, the one dominated by anxiety and negative thoughts.

Gradually, these new habits of calm and serenity will replace the old habits of worry and stress. Thus, day by day, you will be transformed into the calm and mentally balanced person you long to be.

CHAPTER 7
Breathing

"The human body is a marvelous machine, and breathing is its vital force."

Leonardo da Vinci

DIEGO HAD BEEN PRACTICING *martial arts for some time. He stood out for his strength and dexterity. However, something had always prevented him from reaching his full potential: his impatience and anxiety. In every fight, he felt his mind clouded by the pressure, affecting his performance.*

One day, after a particularly frustrating training session, his master, a wise and serene man, called him aside. Noting the restlessness in Diego's eyes, he told him, "To master the art of fighting, you must master your breathing."

Confused but curious, Diego followed the master to a clear area of the dojo. The master invited him into a fighting stance and said, "As you move, Diego, I want you to coordinate every action with your breathing. Inhale deeply when you prepare your attack or defense, and exhale forcefully as you execute the movement."

Diego nodded and began to practice under the teacher's close supervision. Whenever he threw a punch or a kick, he exhaled forcefully, releasing the accumulated tension. Every time he prepared to dodge or block, he inhaled deeply, filling his body with energy. At first, he found it difficult to coordi-

nate his breathing with his movements, but over time, he noticed a change. His previously agitated mind began to calm, and his combat effectiveness increased. He felt a clarity and inner peace that he had never experienced before.

The master continued, "Breathing is the key to keeping your mind calm so you can project your energies at the right time. When you control your breath, you control your mind. And when your mind is at peace, your body can act with precision and strength."

Diego practiced this technique every day, incorporating it into his workouts. Gradually, he noticed how his martial arts performance improved significantly.

That lesson changed his life. Diego understood that true strength lies not only in the muscles but also in the ability to calm the mind and control the breath. Over time, he not only became a better fighter but also a more balanced and calmer person, able to face any adversity with deep breathing and an unflappable spirit.

***

Remember when you were a kid, and you were told to take a deep breath to calm down? Well, it turns out that this piece of popular wisdom has a solid scientific basis. Controlling your breathing not only affects how you feel; it also shapes the structure of your brain in the long run.

Thanks to advances in neuroimaging technology, scientists have discovered which parts of the brain respond to breathing and which do not. And what they've found is shocking. It turns out that not all areas of the brain are activated when you breathe. The most important parts that are activated are the insula, the amygdala, the frontal cortex and the orbitofrontal cortex. These regions are involved in emotion processing, attention and decision-making.

But here's the fascinating part: when you take conscious control of your breathing, these parts of the brain are activated even more. Yes, you read that right. You can directly influence your emotions and alertness simply by paying attention to how you breathe. It's amazing!

This may seem surprising to you, but in reality, Hindu yogis already knew about the power of breathing thousands of years ago. There is an entire branch of yoga called *pranayama*, which is dedicated exclusively to practicing different breathing techniques.

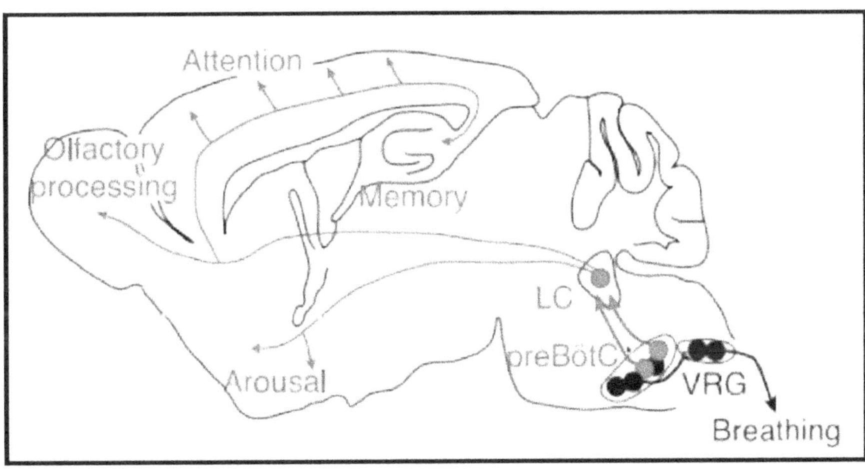

The word *pranayama* comes from Sanskrit and can be translated as "control (Ayama) of the vital force (prana)." These techniques were developed to promote well-being and balance at all levels of being: physical, emotional, mental and spiritual.

So important is this connection between the breath and the brain. In 2017, a research group published in the journal *Science* the first evidence of the anatomical pathways that support it. They decided to call it "*the pranayama pathway*" in honor of this ancient tradition.

It turns out that in the brainstem, right where it connects to the spinal cord, there is something called the *pre-Bötzinger complex,* located in the most primitive brain, in the brainstem. It's a group of neurons responsible for telling the brain how you are breathing at any given moment. Are you breathing through your nose or your mouth? Fast or slow? This complex records all of that!

The research group found a small neuronal subpopulation within the medulla oblongata (a part of the *pre-Bötzinger complex*). Its rhythmic activity is responsible for initiating the breathing process. This group of neurons projects directly to a brain center that controls generalized alertness, attention and stress. So, when you take control of your breathing, you can influence your emotions and your ability to concentrate. Impressive!

The study concluded that breathing affects behavior and higher-order thinking because the pre-bot zinger complex has pathways leading to the locus querulous, then the brain's center for dopamine production. From there, these pathways connect to areas involved in olfactory processing, attention, memory and emotional regulation.

Although the yogis already knew this, it was scientifically demonstrated, for the first time, how breathing influences these parts of the brain.

When you are happy, sad or angry, how you breathe matters too! It's as if your brain uses your breathing to understand your emotions. Therefore, breathing is the language your mind uses to interpret how you feel.

Later, in 2020, a group of researchers embarked on discovering whether the ancient yogic practice of *pranayama* could transform people's brains and moods. To do this, they gathered together a group of people with no previous experience in yoga at the University of Sao Paulo, Brazil.

Before starting their experiment, the scientists meticulously measured the participants' levels of anxiety, emotional regulation and attention by using a cutting-edge technique called "functional magnetic resonance imaging" to examine the participant's brains. It was like drawing a detailed map of each individual's brain activity.

The scientists then divided the participants into two groups: one that would learn the *Bhastrika pranayama* (or bellows breathing technique) and another that would serve as a control group. Both groups were similar in terms of motivation, physical conditions and sociodemographic characteristics, ensuring a fair comparison. The big question was: would the brain activity and mood of those who learned *Bhastrika pranayama* change?

The results were astounding. Although both groups had similar moods at the beginning, after a month of practice, the *pranayama* group showed significant changes in their levels of anxiety and negative emotions: they were more upbeat and positive. It was as if they had found a key to unlock greater happiness and inner peace.

But that wasn't all. When the researchers analyzed their brain activity, they found that the *pranayama* practitioners had increased activity in key areas such as the cingulate cortex and insula, which are responsible for awareness of mental state and emotional regulation. The *pranayama* had turned on lights in areas of the brain that were previously turned off.

But the surprise did not end there. Analysis of neural networks revealed that *pranayama* practice had reshaped the very architecture of the participant's brains. Those who experienced the greatest changes in their cerebral cortex also showed the most significant improvements in their mood.

So, the research showed that the practice of *pranayama* not only improved mood but also physically transformed the brain! It's a powerful tool that is at your fingertips, waiting to be discovered. Are you up for giving it a try and seeing how it can change your life?

All this that you have read, by itself, already justifies the importance of breathing. But I want you to see that the influence of breathing goes much further.

Brain, Attention, Memory and Nasal Breathing

Understanding the relationship between attention and memory is crucial to understanding how your memories work. How can you remember something if you don't even pay attention to it? Because if breathing influences attention, it should also influence memory.

To pay attention and memorize something, your brain needs to coordinate different parts, including the hippocampus, the seahorse-shaped structure that helps you form associations between different experiences and organizes your experiences over time. Without attention, it's difficult for something to be stored in your memory. It's also no coincidence that the hippocampus is one of the areas that is affected by diseases such as Alzheimer's.

When you are with friends, if your attention is divided and you are not really present, your ability to remember that situation is greatly diminished.

According to Harvard research, about 47% of the time you are awake, you are in a state of "autopilot" or lack of conscious presence. This means that your brain remembers where and what you did but does not retain the full experience. It's like having a memory book full of places and dates but without the accompanying emotions and sensations.

This is where breathing plays a key role once again. To have a vivid memory of what you did and what your experience was like, you need to activate the hippocampus in your brain. The hippocampus, in turn, needs to activate the frontal cortex, that region under your forehead that is responsible for paying attention. The way you breathe has a direct impact on this activation.

When you breathe more slowly, the frontal cortex becomes more active, which helps you memorize better. It's as if your brain lights a lamp in that area, allowing you to capture every detail with crystal clarity. In addition, something magical happens: the area of the brain that distracts you, the medial cortex, is turned off when you breathe in this way, as if a switch is turned off. This allows you to stay focused on the present without your mind wandering off to irrelevant thoughts.

These effects have been observed in studies where people are taken to neuroimaging labs and asked to stop breathing for a period of time. In these cases, scientists have noticed that certain areas of the brain are activated, as if lights are switched on in a dashboard. But when they are told to start breathing again, the opposite happens: those lights turn off.

In short, every time you inhale, activity in your frontal cortex increases, while the medial cortex, responsible for distractions, is inhibited. It's as if your breathing is a switch controlling your concentration.

However, you cannot remain exclusively in the frontal cortex, as that would lead to an unhealthy state of hypervigilance. There must be a process of alternation, a back-and-forth between the frontal cortex and the medial cortex.

The breathing cycle is like that of a pendulum swinging between two extremes, yin and yang. This rhythmic movement plays a fundamental role in your ability to pay attention and remember experiences. Ideally, this pendulum should move steadily and harmoniously, like a well-tuned metronome. If the pendulum's movement is too fast or erratic, you come dangerously close to mental chaos.

For your brain to function optimally, it must be activated and deactivated properly. However, many people breathe in a choppy manner and without a steady rhythm, which hinders important mental processes such as attention and memory.

In a study conducted at the University of Madrid, the breathing pattern of 75 participants was examined. Small sensors were placed up their nostrils, and they were asked to breathe. Sounds simple, doesn't it? But what the researchers discovered was shocking. Most of the participants were breathing poorly, unevenly and often through their mouths instead of their noses. Improper breathing patterns hinder the ability to concentrate and remember!

Scientists have conducted fascinating studies over the past decade on how breathing affects your ability to remember. I invite you to participate in one of these experiments. It goes like this: you are shown a series of objects while you breathe. You are then asked which objects you remember. You are more likely to remember the objects you saw as you inhaled compared to those you saw as you exhaled. Not only that, if you breathe in through your mouth, your chances of remembering the objects decrease even more.

But don't be discouraged. The researchers decided to go a step further and train people to breathe through their nose instead of their mouths. After a while, they repeated the tests and voilà! There was a noticeable increase in the participants' memory capacity. It's as if nasal breathing were a magic key that unlocks the doors to your memory!

Breathing and Emotions

In the 1970s, Professors Bloch and Santibañez presented a revealing study at the Latin American Congress on the Psychobiology of Learning, demonstrating how breathing changes according to the emotions you experience. They analyzed a group of participants fitted with chest electrodes. Each basic emotion triggered a different breathing pattern. These are the results they obtained:

- When you feel anger, your inhalations and exhalations are wide, strong and fast. Rage is characterized by wide, nasal, strong inhalations and exhalations and by a decrease in inspiratory time. Rage is rapid but intense.

- Fear causes deep but chaotic breathing. There are no pauses between inspiration and expiration, and the rate of breaths per minute decreases. It is the most difficult emotion to reproduce because of its unpredictable nature.

- Sadness brings paused breathing. Breathing in and breathing out times are longer, with moments of no breathing. The same goes for joy, which, although more accelerated, also presents these blank spaces and involuntary eye movements.

- Tenderness is reflected in a smooth and regular breathing curve without abrupt changes. This is very different from eroticism, where breathing is intensely done through the mouth.

- Sexuality wants to know nothing of the past, only sensations of the present. Mouth breathing predominates. Remember that every time you breathe in through the nose, the areas of the brain most involved in memory are activated.

You need to be clear about how a person in each of these emotional states breathes. Why? Through the execution of the type of breathing that characterizes an emotional state, for example, calmness, you will be able to attract that emotion to your brain and your mind.

Your breath is like a remote control for your emotions. When you learn to recognize and replicate these breathing patterns, you are learning your body's secret language.

It's a skill that will transform your daily life, helping you navigate stressful situations with greater ease and cultivate positive emotional states at will.

Nasal Breathing

Why is breathing through your nose so different from breathing through your mouth? Every time you inhale through your nose, you activate the olfactory bulb in the brain. This small but powerful sensory processing center has a big impact on your emotions and memories.

The remarkable thing is that, of the five senses, smell is the only one with separate neural pathways. So, when you breathe through your nose, you activate the olfactory bulb, even if you don't perceive any odor.

The sense of smell is intimately linked to your memory, being the one that can evoke the most memories. When you breathe through your nose, you keep your olfactory bulb in shape and well trained. And here's the kicker: a healthy olfactory bulb not only improves your ability to remember but also acts as a natural antidepressant and regulates your emotions.

Conversely, those who do not properly activate their olfactory bulb may experience emotional problems. Animal and human studies have shown that inhibition of this structure can lead to symptoms associated with depression.

However, nasal breathing activates not only the olfactory bulb but also other key areas of the brain. The hippocampus is crucial for memory, the amygdala is the center of emotions, and the insula is linked to your personal identity. Therefore, the way you breathe influences not only your affective memory but also your emotional response.

In short, breathing through your nose has a profound impact on your mind and emotions, thanks to the activation of the olfactory bulb and other fundamental brain regions.

Nasal breathing is a simple yet transformative tool that is always at your disposal. So, the next time you want to hold a memory of something or stir an emotion, remember the power of nasal breathing. Take a moment to inhale deeply through your nose, allowing the air to fill your lungs and activate that incredible sensory processing center in your brain.

Inhale and Exhale Rhythms

In a study conducted in Japan, the intriguing connection between nasal breathing and emotions was explored. A group of participants was selected, and their breathing times—specifically, how long they took to inhale and exhale—were measured. These participants were then subjected to a stressful situation, and their reactions were observed. Individuals whose breathing rhythms, under normal conditions, were characterized by short exhalations experienced higher levels of anxiety when faced with a stressful situation.

What does this tell us? It suggests that the way you breathe can predispose your mind and body to certain emotions. It's as if you are training your brain, day in and day out, through your breathing pattern. When faced with a stressful situation, the body tends to replicate the behavior or habit created through repetition. When a stressful moment occurs, your brain automatically triggers the emotional response associated with that breathing rhythm. It's a deeply ingrained habit, reinforced by myelin-coated neural circuits.

But here comes the important part: you have the power to change this cycle.

Subsequently, the same group of people was taught to exhale more slowly, calmly and in control. Then, they were exposed to a different stressful situation than before. What do you think happened? Their emotional reaction was noticeably different. Through conscious breathing, they managed to regulate their emotions effectively.

This study is strong evidence that modifying the breathing pattern has a significant impact on emotion regulation in stressful situations. While anxiety is a complex emotion influenced by many factors, do not underestimate the power of your breath as a tool for managing it.

Many people exhale abruptly as if they were releasing all their tension in a single breath. But this way of exhaling has a negative impact on your brain. Think of your brain like an orchestra. It needs time to activate and deactivate different systems harmoniously and rhythmically. When you exhale sharply, it's as if you are taking the conductor's baton away, leaving the musicians without guidance. It's because of this that it's no wonder so many people feel unbalanced and out of tune with themselves. Much of this imbalance can be attributed to the poor way they breathe. They are depriving the brain of the rhythm it needs to function optimally.

Regarding emotions, the length of your inhalation and exhalation plays a crucial role.

We've already talked about how important it is to breathe in through your nose. Now, pay special attention to your exhalation. When it comes to exhaling, your brain is less concerned with whether you exhale through your nose or your mouth. What really counts is how much time you spend on each exhalation.

If you want to calm your emotions, you can do two things:

1. Reduce the Number of Breaths you Take Per Minute

This decreases emotional response and calms your mind.

Start by paying attention to your breathing rate. How many breaths do you take per minute? If you normally take 12 breaths, try gradually reducing that number. The goal is not to force it or cause discomfort but to let your breathing naturally slow down and deepen.

2. Double the Time of Your Exhalation

On your next inhalation, mentally count to 2. Then, as you exhale, extend the count to 4. Inhale again for 2 seconds and exhale for 4. Repeat this breathing pattern: 2-4-2-4. Inhale peace, exhale tension. Inhale calm, exhale anxiety.

It may seem simple, but this breathing rhythm has a profound impact on your nervous system. By extending the length of your exhalation, you are sending a direct signal to your brain, especially to the amygdala, a small but powerful structure that is responsible for your emotional responses.

When you exhale longer, the amygdala calms down. It's as if you're telling it, "Everything's fine, there's no danger, you can relax." Your brain listens and responds accordingly, decreasing the production of stress hormones and allowing your body to enter a state of calm and balance. This breathing pattern will help you balance your nervous system and maintain a state of calm and mental clarity, even in times of extremely high stress or anxiety.

This is not just a theory; it is a fact that science has proven. In laboratory experiments, it has been shown that when people slow down their breathing and prolong the exhalation to twice as long as the inspiration, their emotions are soothed. The key is this extended exhalation time, which acts as a natural brake on the amygdala and intense emotional responses.

Influence of Breathing on Heart Rate

Now that you understand the deep connection between your breathing and your emotions, it's time to delve into how this link extends to your heart rate variability and how you can harness it to lower your anxiety levels and also make more energy available if you need it.

Your heart works in sync with your breathing. With each inhalation, your diaphragm, that dome-shaped muscle below your lungs, lowers to make room for your expanding lungs. At this point, your heart also expands slightly, causing blood to flow more slowly through the increased volume. Your brain, ever vigilant, quickly sends a signal to your heart to speed up its rhythm and adapt to this change.

In short, inhaling speeds up the heart.

Now, when you exhale, the opposite happens. Your diaphragm rises, reducing the space in your chest cavity. Your heart contracts a little, blood moves faster through the smaller volume, and your brain signals your heart to slow down its rhythm.

In short, exhaling slows down the heart.

Doctors call this process "respiratory sinus arrhythmia," and it's the basis of what we call "heart rate variability" (HRV).

Here's the key, and I want you to remember it because it reinforces what you have learned: when you emphasize your exhalations, making them longer than your inhalations, you lower your heart rate and calm your nervous system.

On the other hand, when you emphasize your inhalations and make them more vigorous or longer than your exhalations, you speed up your heart rate and quicken your nervous system.

With this knowledge, imagine you find yourself in a stressful situation, perhaps an important meeting or an anxiety attack. Instead of allowing your heart rate to skyrocket and your emotions to overwhelm you, you can simply focus on lengthening your exhalations, allowing them to be longer than your inhalations. In doing so, you will be sending a direct signal to your heart and nervous system to calm down and balance.

Conversely, you can emphasize your inhalations if you need a boost of energy and vitality, making them deeper and more vigorous, allowing them to be longer than your exhalations. This will speed up your heart rate and give you that extra boost you need.

In short, when you inhale, especially if you inhale through your nose, your brain is activated (yang), while when you exhale, whether through your nose or mouth, your brain is inhibited (yin). If you breathe through your mouth when you inhale, your amygdala is not aware of it, which can be beneficial in inducing a state of relaxation in cases of extreme stress.

***

Now, let's move on to the practical part, where all of the above is summarized. I will teach you a few breathing tools to apply to your life. Some will be for you to incorporate on a regular basis, such as the conscious breathing technique, and others will be there for you to apply in certain situations when you need them most.

Tool 1: Conscious Breathing

I will now give you a clear and concise breakdown of how to breathe, although I advise you not to become obsessed with the technique. What is important is that you are aware of your breathing and that you practice it regularly.

Most people do not use their full lung capacity; they do shallow breathing, preventing good oxygenation. You probably do the same without realizing it.

There are three types of breathing: abdominal, thoracic and clavicular. CONSCIOUS BREATHING is the integration of the three into one. To achieve it, you must follow these steps:

Step 1. Abdominal Breathing

When you breathe in, fill the lower part of the lungs with air, moving the diaphragm downwards and causing the belly to come out. You will feel your abdomen swell. Concentrate on this sensation and keep your attention on it for a few breaths.

Step 2. Thoracic or Intercostal Breathing

In the next phase, the air should penetrate the thoracic region, specifically the rib area. Feel your ribs expand laterally as you inhale. Hold this breath for a few moments, being fully aware of the sensations it generates.

Step 3. Clavicular Breathing

Finally, complete the breath by filling the upper part of the lungs, concentrating on the collarbone area. Notice how this area rises slightly at the end of the inhalation. Hold the air briefly before you begin to exhale slowly.

Practice integrating these three phases of breathing smoothly and continuously. Over time, you will find it to be a natural process that you can apply whenever you need to relax or focus on the present.

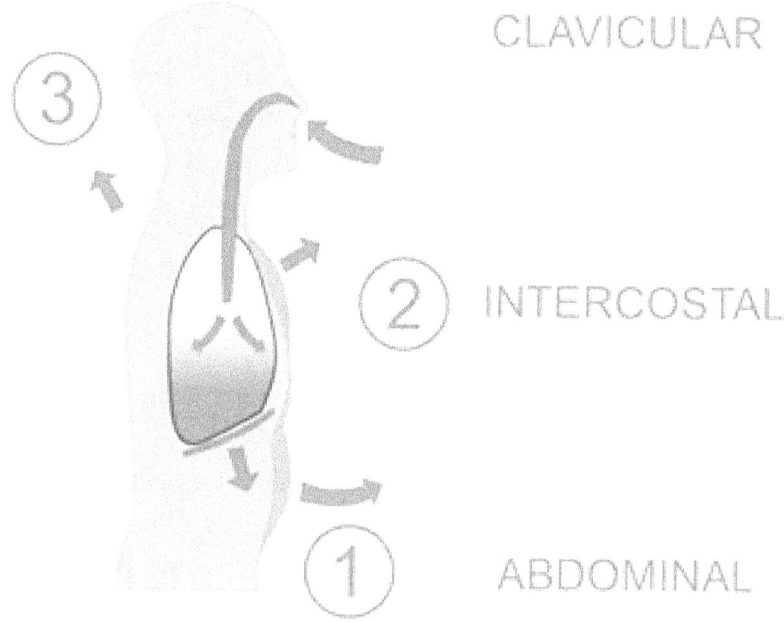

Now, practice integrating these three phases of breathing. Start by lying on your back, allowing your body to relax completely. Once you are comfortable with the technique in this position, move on to practicing it in a seated position. Keep your spine straight but relaxed and continue to integrate the three phases of breathing.

With regular practice, this way of breathing will become instinctive and the basis for any type of breathing technique you wish to practice. Always remember to listen to your body and move at your own pace, enjoying the benefits of full and conscious breathing.

First, you must begin by emptying your lungs with a deep exhalation. Then:

1. Breathe in slowly, gently and deeply; feel how the air is directed towards the abdomen. Let air into the lower area of the lungs as the diaphragm descends. The abdominal area swells, but not in an exaggerated way. It should be a relaxed inspiration but with control of the abdominal waist.

2. When the lower part of the lungs is full of air, dilate the ribs without forcing them, allowing even more air to enter the lungs. With your hand resting on the ribs, you should notice how the ribs separate.

3. When the ribs are separated to the maximum, raise the clavicles without raising the shoulders to let in even more air and finish filling the lungs completely. During the whole process of inspiration, the air should enter progressively, without jolts, smoothly and continuously.

The exhalation is carried out in the opposite direction, always smoothly and slowly, without abruptness or effort, emptying first the upper part of the lungs.

- First, the upper part of the lungs (clavicular breathing),

- Then the chest (thoracic breathing), which deflates,

- And, finally, the belly (abdominal breathing), which descends until the last remaining air comes out.

No noise should be made when breathing. It is essential to breathe softly and quietly. Both exhalation and inspiration should be silent, slow, continuous and comfortable, without ever forcing.

All conscious attention should be on the act of breathing so that the three movements of the complete breath are clearly discernible but harmoniously integrated. Conscious breathing should not cause discomfort or fatigue. In fact, it can be exercised as much as one wishes at any time.

And I repeat, once again, the important thing is not so much that you do a perfect technique as that you manage to breathe in a harmonious and fluid way, allowing oxygen to enter the lower or abdominal part of the body.

I will now clearly and concisely break down a series of anti-anxiety tools based on breathing for you so that you can include them in your program.

Tool 2: Alternate Breathing. Balancing Brain Hemispheres

Dedicating just a few minutes a day to alternate breathing, known as *Nadi Shodhan pranayama*, is the key to relieving stress, tension and accumulated fatigue. By practicing this technique regularly, you will not only cleanse and unblock the energy channels in your body but also effectively calm your mind and balance the use of both brain hemispheres. You will notice how you gradually feel more relaxed, centered and with greater mental clarity.

Sit comfortably with a straight spine and relaxed shoulders, or lie down comfortably with a straight spine.

Keep a gentle smile on your face.

Close your eyes and begin to breathe gently through your nose without forcing your breath, allowing your body to let go with each exhalation. Do not breathe through your mouth or make noise. Feel how, little by little, you are entering a state of calm and serenity while you concentrate only on the natural flow of your breath.

Place your fingers gently on your forehead and nose without pressing too hard.

Use your dominant hand and place your index and middle finger between your eyebrows, just where the bridge of your nose begins. Next, place the ring and little fingers on the left nostril, slightly covering it. Finally, place the thumb on the right nostril, gently covering the opening. Hold this finger position while breathing, allowing the breath to flow naturally through the spaces between your fingers.

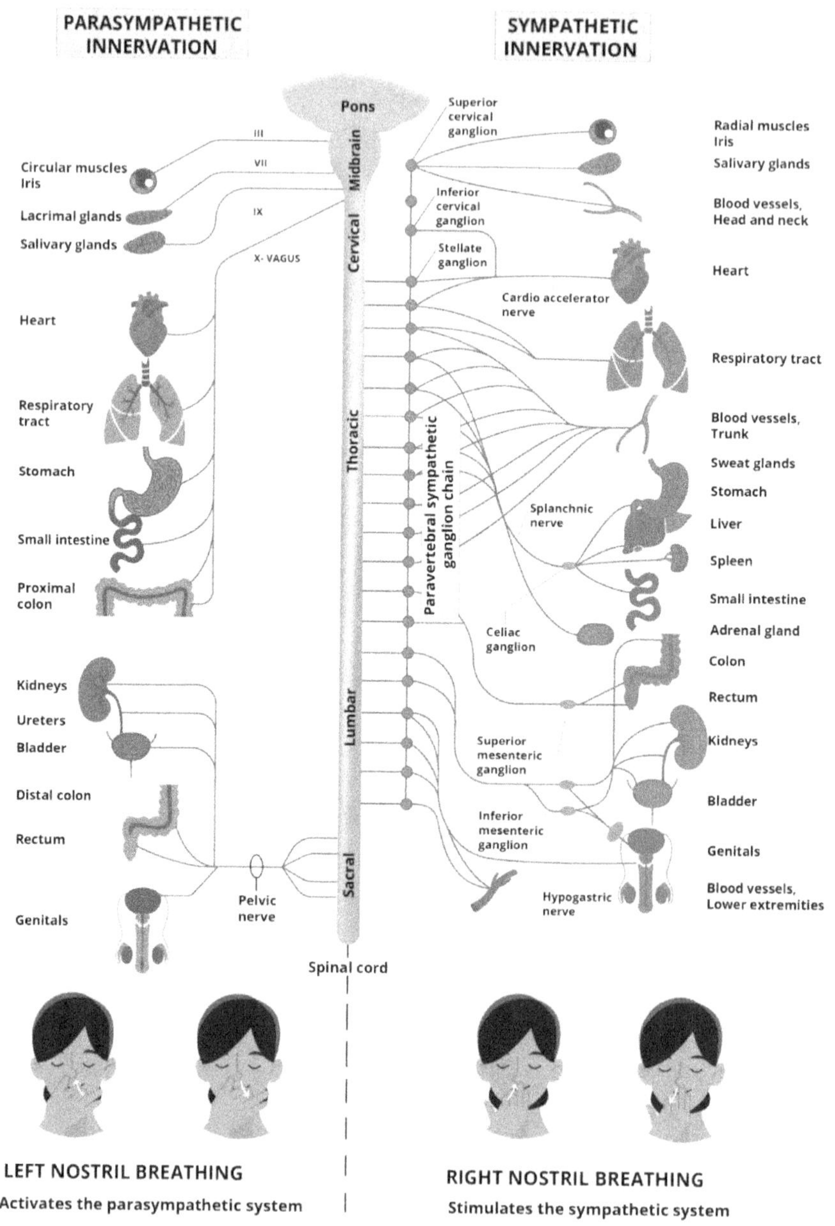
PARASYMPATHETIC INNERVATION
SYMPATHETIC INNERVATION
Pons
Midbrain
III
VII
IX
X- VAGUS
Circular muscles Iris
Lacrimal glands
Salivary glands
Heart
Respiratory tract
Stomach
Small intestine
Proximal colon
Kidneys
Ureters
Bladder
Distal colon
Rectum
Genitals
Pelvic nerve
Spinal cord
Cervical
Thoracic
Lumbar
Sacral
Paravertebral sympathetic ganglion chain
Superior cervical ganglion
Inferior cervical ganglion
Stellate ganglion
Cardio accelerator nerve
Splanchnic nerve
Celiac ganglion
Superior mesenteric ganglion
Inferior mesenteric ganglion
Hypogastric nerve
Radial muscles Iris
Salivary glands
Blood vessels, Head and neck
Heart
Respiratory tract
Blood vessels, Trunk
Sweat glands
Stomach
Liver
Spleen
Small intestine
Adrenal gland
Colon
Rectum
Kidneys
Bladder
Genitals
Blood vessels, Lower extremities
LEFT NOSTRIL BREATHING
Activates the parasympathetic system
RIGHT NOSTRIL BREATHING
Stimulates the sympathetic system

Breathing Exercise

Gently close your right nostril with your thumb and breathe in through your left nostril, allowing air to fill your lungs.

Feel your abdomen expand with each inhalation.

Then, gently close your left nostril with your ring and little finger, and exhale slowly through your right nostril as you remove your thumb.

Let the air come out naturally without forcing it.

Next, inhale deeply through the right nostril, filling your lungs again.

Finally, exhale in a controlled manner through the left nostril, completing a round of alternate breathing.

Continue this process for a total of 10 rounds, keeping your eyes closed at all times. Concentrate on breathing deeply and effortlessly, making sure that each exhalation has the same duration as the inhalation.

Allow your body to relax with each breathing cycle, releasing any accumulated tension.

Tool 3: Basic Relaxing Rhythmic Breathing. Accentuating the Exhalation. *Bhramari Pranayama* Breathing Technique

Concentrate on the following breathing pattern:

- Empty the lungs of air.

- Breathe in silently through the nose for 4 seconds.

- Hold your breath for 4 seconds.

- Exhale through your mouth, closing your lips and making a "whooshing." noise, for 8 seconds.

- Repeat the cycle up to 10 times.

Bhramari pranayama, also called bee buzzing breathing, is a technique that unites sound and breath. This technique can be performed in a simple or more advanced way. For now, we will start with the easy one.

Sitting in a comfortable posture that allows you to raise your spine, inhale slowly and deeply through your nose using the necessary supports. Keep your lips gently sealed on the exhalation, in contact but without forcing, and make the "m" sound. A sound similar to the buzzing of a bee will be produced.

Let the sound be soft and balanced in intensity and tonality.

The exhalation will naturally be longer than the inhalation. Do not be in a hurry to inhale again; do it slowly and smoothly. On the next exhalation, produce the "mmm" sound again.

Keep your eyes closed and your face relaxed and allow yourself to concentrate on the sound you produce. Look for a natural and comfortable sound.

Continue.

If it is comfortable, you can place your thumbs or index fingers over your ear holes so that the vibration produced by your own sound expands.

You can practice this for as long as necessary. The mind will concentrate on the sound. Slow breathing will cause the nervous system to relax. When you finish, keep your eyes closed, your posture spacious and soft, and keep your concentration.

The practice of this technique will bring you a variety of benefits, among them:

- Eases mental tension, anxiety, stress or anger.

- Stimulates the parasympathetic nervous system.

- Induces muscle relaxation.

- It may be useful in preparation for childbirth or during labor.

- It may help calm babies after birth when they need to sleep or are agitated.

- Useful in preparation for meditation, helping to concentrate the mind.

- It can help in a state of insomnia, especially if you do it before going to sleep.

- By vibration in the chest, throat and skull can clarify these areas physically, emotionally and energetically.

Tool 4: Relaxing Breath of Urgency: Accentuating the Exhalation

When you find yourself in a situation of sudden stress that makes you lose control, and you need to quickly reduce the tension, do the following:

- Breathe in quickly, filling your lungs.

- Then breathe out slowly, lengthening the exhalation as much as you can. It doesn't matter if you double or triple the time of your exhalation.

- Breathe in again quickly, filling your lungs well.

- Breathe out again slowly, smoothly and extending as much as you can.

Repeat this breathing pattern as many times as necessary. Remember that lengthening the exhalation will relax your heart, and you will send a clear sign to the brain of calm and tranquility.

You may feel the effects in a matter of seconds, or it may take longer.

Don't give up, keep going because the triumph is yours!

CHAPTER 8

Physical Exercise

"Mens sana in corpore sano."

Juvenal

MARINA AWOKE WITH A *start. Her heart was pounding, and she had a feeling of tightness in her chest that was all too familiar. It wasn't the first time anxiety had assaulted her in the middle of the night, but this time, she felt something had to change.*

She sat up in bed and tried to calm her breathing. She remembered her therapist's words, "Physical exercise can be an excellent tool for managing your anxiety."

Until now, she had put off the idea—she didn't have the time or energy for it. But that morning, something in her decided she had to give it a try.

With determination, Marina got up, dressed in sports clothes she hadn't worn in years and went outside. The fresh morning air caressed her face, and the nearby park seemed like a good place to start.

At first, she felt ridiculous, running awkwardly as if everyone were watching her. But little by little, the rhythm of her steps became synchronized with her breathing.

At that hour, Madrid's Buen Retiro Park unfolded before her like an oasis of tranquility in the middle of the hectic city. She passed the Palacio de Cristal; the glass walls reflected the dawn light. She then passed the central pond, where the first rowers of the day were already in their boats. The park's atmosphere, with its century-old fountains and statues, gave her a new feeling.

As she ran, her mind cleared. The thoughts that usually overwhelmed her began to fade away, leaving room for an unfamiliar and pleasant mental silence. Worries about work, conflicts with her family, and the constant fear of the future faded away, replaced by the effect of movement.

As she completed her first lap of the park, she stopped, exhausted but strangely revitalized. As she caught her breath, she realized that her mind was calm for the first time in a long time.

Days turned into weeks, and running became routine. Marina began to notice subtle changes in her life. She was sleeping better, she felt more focused at work, and, most importantly, anxiety was beginning to lose its grip on her. In addition, she joined a group of runners, finding in them an unexpected source of support and friendship.

One morning, while she was running with her new friends, one of them, Alex, told her about participating in a race, the popular San Silvestre Vallecana, which is held every December 31. The idea of participating in such an event intimidated her but also excited her. Ultimately, she decided to sign up, seeing it as a personal challenge and a way of thanking physical exercise for having helped her so much.

On race day, Marina felt nervous but also prepared. Then she remembered her first park run and how her life had changed since then.

When the starting gun sounded, Marina ran with all her heart. As she crossed the finish line, amidst applause and smiles, she knew her life would never be the same again. She had learned to run not just to escape anxiety but to find herself, and in the process, she had discovered an inner strength she never imagined she had.

***

Imagine a magic pill that not only reduces anxiety but also improves your mood, increases your energy, and makes you feel more optimistic about life. That pill exists, and it's called physical exercise. With every step you take and every muscle you move, you are releasing powerful chemicals in your brain that naturally and effectively fight anxiety.

Numerous scientific studies have conclusively shown that regular physical activity significantly reduces the symptoms of anxiety.

For example, a study published in the prestigious journal The Lancet Psychiatry revealed that people who exercise regularly are 43% less likely to experience episodes of anxiety. This means that by incorporating exercise into your daily routine, you're taking a step toward protecting your mental and emotional well-being. You don't need to be an elite athlete or spend hours in the gym to reap these benefits. Even a brisk 30-minute walk a day can do wonders to calm your mind and elevate your mood.

Why Exercise Is Good for You

Now that we've established that exercise is good for both the body and mind, we must ask: why exactly? How does it achieve this, and what type of exercise is most effective?

When you do cardiovascular exercise on a regular basis, you are basically creating symptoms of anxiety in your body: sweating, shortness of breath and palpitations. But don't panic because this is a good thing. By repeating this regularly, you get used to these sensations and your resting heart rate self-compensates and slows down. This, in turn, signals to your brain a sense of internal calm, ultimately reducing your overall anxiety

You've probably heard of the famous "runner's high," which describes a phenomenon where, after intense aerobic exercise such as running, you may experience a feeling of euphoria and well-being. For years, it was thought that this was exclusively due to the release of endorphins, the body's natural opiates. Yes, you indeed get a release of endorphins with exercise, which serves to reduce the perception of pain during and after intense activity. But those endorphins are not the only ones that affect you or your brain and mood the most because they do not cross the blood-brain barrier. In fact, your brain is very selective about what it allows through.

It's known that anyone can experience a feeling of relaxation after moderately intense exercise, not from endorphins, but from endocannabinoids.

The positive feelings you get after exercise are due to the release of endocannabinoids that cross the blood-brain barrier. Endocannabinoids are substances your body produces that activate cannabinoid receptors in your body.

Marijuana

Over the past two decades, society has paid a lot of attention to marijuana. In early 2023, it was legalized for recreational use in 21 U.S. states, and its use for medical purposes has grown significantly over the past 20 years. Marijuana has gone from being a taboo subject to being a topic of conversation and accepted in many places.

The important thing to know is that your body naturally produces chemicals similar to delta-9-tetrahydrocannabinol, or THC, the psychoactive compound in marijuana that comes from the Cannabis sativa plant. These substances are endocannabinoids and are found in all vertebrate species. In simpler terms, your own body has an internal system that influences your mood, appetite, pain and other physiological functions.

When you're exercising vigorously, it's as if you're creating your own strain of cannabis within your body, as your homemade cannabinoids have a positive effect on your mood and reduce your anxiety.

The two most studied cannabinoids you produce internally are AEA and 2-AG. I'll spare you the full names, but the "A" stands for arachidonic acid. These compounds interact with cannabinoid receptors in your brain and body, triggering a cascade of beneficial effects.

When you exercise intensely, your body releases these endocannabinoids in greater quantities, which can lead you to experience a sense of euphoria and well-being. So, the next time you're feeling stressed or anxious, remember that you have the power to harness your own endocannabinoid system and improve your mood naturally through vigorous exercise.

But there's more. Regular exercise has a prolonged effect on improving mood and stress levels because it triggers brain-derived neurotrophic factor (BDNF), which causes neurogenesis, the growth of new cells and regeneration of damaged cells.

BDNF is part of a family of proteins known as neurotrophins, which are vital for the survival, development and function of neurons in your brain. This protein is found in several key regions, including the hippocampus, cerebral cortex and basal forebrain.

These regions are involved in fundamental processes such as learning, memory and emotional regulation. The more BDNF you have circulating in these areas, the better you will be able to learn, remember and healthily manage your emotions.

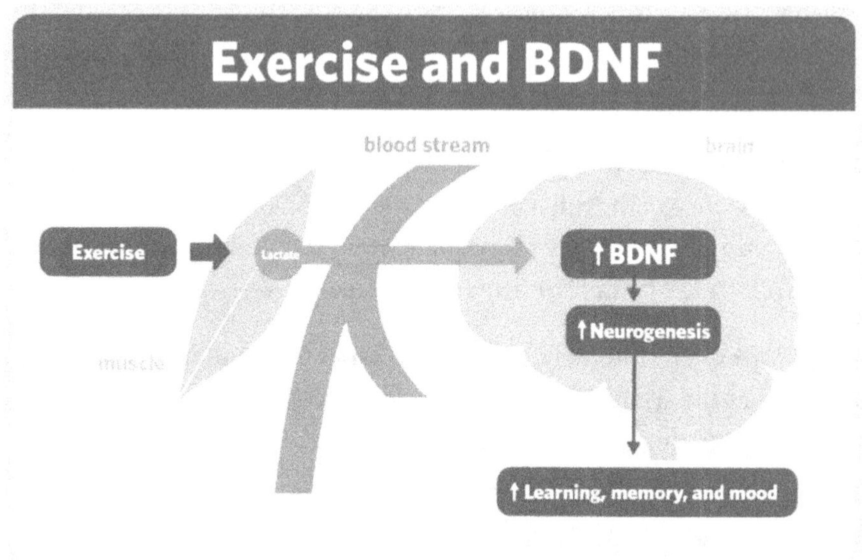

Anxiety is often associated with low levels of BDNF. Studies have shown that people who suffer from anxiety disorders often exhibit lower levels of BDNF compared to those without these disorders. This suggests that BDNF protects against anxiety, possibly by promoting neurogenesis and synaptic plasticity.

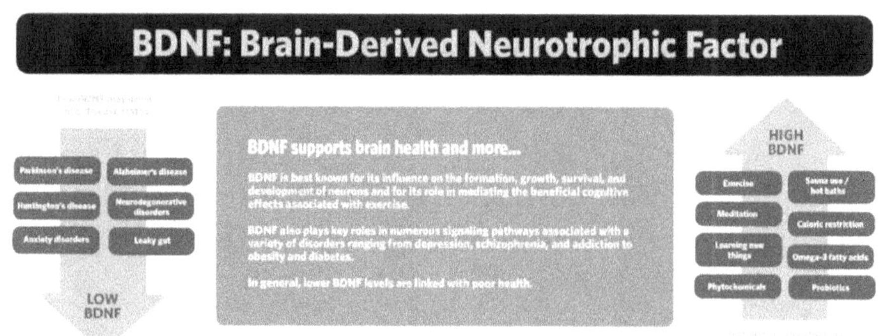

How to Stimulate BDNF Production

Exercise is one of the best ways to stimulate your BDNF production and keep your brain functioning in optimal condition. For this reason, people who practice sports regularly have larger hippocampus structures due to this neurogenesis. And when it comes to brains, you want a big hippocampus. A small hippocampus is considered an indicator of depression.

What kind of exercise can help you get this big hippocampus? Studies recommend 150 minutes a week of moderate-intensity exercise and 75 minutes a week of high-intensity exercise.

You should be able to talk with moderate intensity but not very easily. Examples of moderate exercise are brisk walking at three miles per hour, cycling at a leisurely pace, dancing, or playing doubles tennis with friends. So, if you're walking your dog or gardening and you can sing or whistle a tune with no problem, you're probably not doing it hard enough to get the maximum benefits for your brain and your overall health. Try increasing the pace a bit until you notice your breathing quickens and you find it harder to carry on a flowing conversation.

You won't be able to talk at high intensity because you'll be breathing too hard. Examples of this are running at a pace of about ten kilometers per hour, which would be equivalent to running one kilometer in six minutes, swimming in lanes, or participating in some aerobics classes, depending on how intense the workout is.

You can divide these times however you prefer, but it is advisable to spread it out over the week; for example, do 30 minutes on a treadmill five times a week for a moderate workout or do a 15-minute fast-paced cycling session five times a week. The important thing is to find a balance that fits your routine and allows you to maintain consistency in your physical activity.

Now, any type of activity is better than no activity at all. So, a slow walk around your neighborhood still benefits you, but you need some aerobic and anaerobic activity to activate the endocannabinoid system and increase neurogenesis.

In short, activities such as running, swimming and cycling are particularly effective in increasing BDNF levels. Increased blood flow and oxygenation of the brain during aerobic exercise stimulate the production of this neurotrophic factor.

Weightlifting and other forms of strength training have also been shown to increase BDNF levels. So don't hesitate to supplement your cardio routine with some weight training sessions. You'll strengthen not only your muscles but your mind as well.

With neurogenesis, there is an effect of increased dopamine and serotonin, neurotransmitters that improve mood. Serotonin plays a crucial role in regulating your sleep cycle. Better sleep contributes to you experiencing less anxiety and greater overall well-being. Regular exercise, therefore, will help you normalize your sleep patterns by increasing your serotonin levels.

This means that when you exercise regularly, you are not only strengthening your body but also your mind. You're stimulating the growth of new brain cells and increasing the levels of neurotransmitters that make you feel good. Every step you take, every push-up you do, and every lap you swim contributes to creating a healthier brain. Your dedication to physical exercise translates directly into greater mental clarity, better stress management and a more positive outlook on life's challenges.

✳✳✳

Now that you've seen how sport can be your best ally in the fight against anxiety, it's time to break down the different types of exercise you can do so you can create your personalized weekly program.

Discover how each modality can help you find the balance and wellness you crave.

Whether you prefer endurance activities, strength training or relaxing practices like yoga, there's a perfect option for you.

Get ready to dive into the fascinating world of fitness and discover how each type of exercise can transform your life, reducing stress and filling you with positive energy.

Moderate Intensity or Aerobic Exercise: Running, Swimming, Cycling

Aerobic exercise is a moderate-intensity physical activity performed with sufficient oxygen to meet the body's energy demands for an extended period. The term "aerobic" means "with oxygen," and this type of exercise is characterized by rhythmic, continuous movements that can be maintained over the long term. It increases heart rate and respiration sustainably.

Running, swimming, or moderate-intensity cycling are ideal for fighting anxiety and should be the foundation of your program.

High Intensity or Anaerobic Exercise: Weightlifting, Strength Training or Running and

Swimming at High Intensity

Anaerobic exercise is a high-intensity physical activity performed in short periods of time and with an energy demand that exceeds the available oxygen supply. The term "anaerobic" means "without oxygen," and this type of exercise primarily uses glycogen stored in the muscles as a source of energy.

Running, swimming or cycling, if performed at a high intensity and cannot be sustained over the long term, become anaerobic exercises. These exercises improve power and speed.

Weight work can also be included. Anaerobic work at a higher intensity than aerobic should complement aerobic work in your program, which should always be the foundation.

Intense exercise promotes the production of lactate, a by-product of glucose metabolism. Your body "transports" lactate from your muscles to various tissues, such as your heart and brain, serving as a source of energy. Once in your brain, lactate acts as a signaling molecule to activate BDNF production.

Lactate is crucial for raising BDNF levels, and high-intensity interval training is markedly more effective than moderate continuous exercise at increasing BDNF.

Moderate to vigorous intensity exercise (at least 65% of maximum heart rate) for approximately 40 minutes showed the greatest effects on BDNF levels in a group of young, healthy men. The BDNF level increased by almost one-third after exercise.

However, both types of exercise are important for cardiovascular health and form a balanced fitness routine. While aerobic exercise improves endurance and overall heart health, anaerobic exercise strengthens muscles and increases the ability to perform high-intensity activities. Combining both into your routine is the key to achieving optimal health and a balanced mind.

Flexibility and Balance Exercise: Yoga, Pilates, Tai-Chi, Dancing

This type of exercise will also be very helpful to you, and you should practice some of it two or three times a week. Through controlled movements and deep breathing, yoga and Pilates teach you to be present in the moment, reducing anxiety and stress. In a yoga class, each posture connects you with yourself, while a Pilates session leaves you feeling more aligned and centered. These practices improve your flexibility and strength and give you tools to manage anxiety, turning each session into a haven of peace.

Team or Social Sports: Soccer, Basketball, tennis, etc.

Last but not least are team sports. In them, you get the benefits that are already mentioned but from a playful point of view. You play, you have fun, and you stay active. Soccer, basketball and other similar sports keep you physically active and provide you with a social support network. The camaraderie and team spirit that develops in these sports are crucial in combating anxiety. Being surrounded by peers who share your goals and support you every step of the way creates a sense of belonging and community that can be incredibly therapeutic.

In short, no matter what type of exercise you choose, each has its magic. From the exhilaration of a sunrise run to the tranquility of a yoga class, the strength of lifting weights, and the camaraderie of a team sport, there's a perfect fit for every person and every situation. So why not try them all and find out which one is best for you? Your mind and body will thank you!

Physical Exercise Tool: Include Some of These Habits in Your Life

Cardiovascular (combines moderate and high intensities): walking, running, cycling, swimming.

Yoga: Yoga combines physical movements with breathing techniques and meditation, which can help calm the mind and reduce anxiety. Yoga postures (asanas) and breathing sequences (*pranayama*) can improve flexibility, reduce muscle tension and promote relaxation.

Tai-Chi or Qi-Gong: Tai-chi or Qi-Gong is a gentle exercise that combines slow, flowing movements with deep breathing and relaxation techniques.

Karate, Kung-Fu: You can practice a martial art that will strengthen your body and mind.

Pilates: Pilates is an exercise system that focuses on strengthening the core muscles of the body, improving posture and promoting flexibility.

Strength Training: Strength training is done either with weights, resistance machines, or your own body weight.

Dance: A fun and effective form of exercise. In addition, dancing promotes emotional expression and social connection, which can also reduce anxiety.

Social sports: Soccer, basketball, tennis, etc.

CHAPTER 9
Nutrition and Diet

Hippocrates

JAVIER WAS A YOUNG finance professional living in the bustling city of Madrid. His life was fast-paced, with long days at the office and endless social engagements. He didn't pay much attention to his diet, often resorting to fast food and unhealthy snacks to satisfy her hunger between meetings.

One afternoon, while preparing for an important presentation at work, Javier began to feel severe chest pain, shortness of breath and a distressing sense of panic. Thinking he was having a heart attack, he was rushed to the hospital. After several tests, the doctors explained that he had suffered a panic attack.

This episode was a turning point for Javier. He realized that his body was sending him signals that something was wrong. He decided to visit a nutritionist, Maria, to see if his diet could be contributing to his problems.

Maria gave him a thorough examination and asked him several questions about his eating habits. The results revealed several nutritional deficiencies: low in magnesium, vitamin B deficiency and insufficient levels of omega-3 fatty acids. Maria explained that these deficiencies could significantly affect his nervous system and contribute to his panic attacks and anxiety.

With a clear plan in mind, Javier began to change his diet. He incorporated magnesium-rich foods such as almonds and spinach, increased his intake of B vitamins with whole grains and green leafy vegetables, and added fatty fish such as salmon for omega-3s. He also reduced his caffeine and sugar intake, opting for healthier choices.

Within a few weeks, Javier noticed a marked improvement. He felt calmer, his energy levels were more stable, and he never had another panic attack. In addition, his work performance improved, and his mind was clearer.

Javier understood that nutrition was a fundamental tool for his mental well-being. His experience taught him to take better care of his body and listen to its signals.

***

The connection between what you eat and how you feel is more than evident. In the hustle and bustle of modern life, it's easy to overlook the importance of a balanced diet, especially when faced with the constant pressure of work, social commitments and personal responsibilities.

"Let your food be your medicine, and your medicine be your food," said Hippocrates, the ancient sage and father of medicine. This insight still holds today. Food is the fuel you need for your daily activities and the foundation on which your physical and mental health is built.

For centuries, different cultures and traditions have recognized food's preventive and healing power. In Chinese medicine, diet is fundamental to maintaining balance and health. In the Ayurvedic tradition of India, food is known to nourish the body and influence the mind and spirit. These ancient wisdoms teach us that proper nutrition prevents disease, increases our energy and improves our quality of life.

Modern science supports this ancient knowledge. Recent research has shown that a balanced diet that does not include processed foods and is rich in fruits, vegetables, whole grains, fish, and nuts improves physical health and reduces stress and anxiety. Essential nutrients such as vitamins, minerals and antioxidants play a crucial role in the functioning of the brain and immune system.

Incorporating healthy foods into your diet is an effective and natural way to care for yourself. It's not just about avoiding disease; it's about living with more vitality and balance. You are investing in your future well-being by choosing unprocessed, fresh and nutritious foods.

So, remember Hippocrates's words and ancient traditions the next time you plan your meals. Make your diet a priority. Your body and mind will thank you.

Numerous research studies have shown that what we eat influences our mental health.

According to Dr. Felice Jacka, a pioneer in nutritional psychiatry, what you eat is critical to your mental health. In her article *"Nutritional Psychiatry: Where to next?"* published in *EBioMedicine*, she reveals how diet profoundly influences emotional well-being.

Polyphenols

Polyphenols are a large family of organic compounds present in many foods you probably consume regularly, such as fruits, vegetables, tea, wine and cocoa. Within this group are flavonoids, a specific type of polyphenols that stand out for their various beneficial effects on your health.

These flavonoids act as powerful antioxidants, helping to protect your cells from damage caused by free radicals. In addition, they possess anti-inflammatory properties that help reduce inflammation in your body and brain.

By increasing your intake of fruits and vegetables rich in flavonoids, you can increase the levels of BDNF in your blood.

A delicious cup of cocoa is rich in flavonoids. With each sip, you'll be filling your body with 494 milligrams of these powerful compounds. Gradually, without you even realizing it, the levels of BDNF in your blood will begin to rise.

Dietary Patterns

The typical Western diet, rich in simple carbohydrates and saturated fats, depletes BDNF levels in the body. Regular consumption of processed foods, refined sugars, and fast food decreases the production of this essential protein for mental well-being.

When adults with metabolic syndrome followed a low-carbohydrate diet for four weeks (about 40 percent fewer calories than usual), their BDNF levels increased by 20 percent.

Whole grains, such as oats, quinoa and brown rice, are excellent sources of sustained energy. Unlike refined carbohydrates, which cause abrupt rises and falls in blood sugar levels, whole grains release glucose slowly and steadily. This keeps your energy and mood stable, helping you face daily challenges with more serenity. Maintaining stable blood glucose levels is crucial to avoid mood swings and anxiety.

Omega-3 Fatty Acids

Fish, especially varieties rich in omega-3 fatty acids such as salmon, mackerel and sardines, are also essential for brain health. Studies have shown that omega-3s reduce levels of the stress hormone cortisol and promote a calmer, more balanced state of mind. In addition, omega-3s are essential components of neuron cell membranes, facilitating communication between brain cells and improving cognitive functioning.

Three omega-3 fatty acids are essential for human health: alpha-linolenic acid (ALA), eicosapentaenoic acid (EPA) and docosahexaenoic acid (DHA). ALA is found in vegetable oils, such as walnuts and flaxseed oils. EPA and DHA are found in meat and fats from fish and marine animals. EPA and DHA from marine sources are particularly potent in enhancing brain-derived neurotrophic factors, which are key players in brain health and cognitive function.

Magnesium and Vitamin B

Nuts and seeds are true superfoods for the brain. Rich in magnesium, zinc and healthy fatty acids, these little wonders can greatly impact your mental health. Magnesium, in particular, is known for its nervous system relaxing properties. A study published in the *Journal of Affective Disorders* found that adequate magnesium intake is associated with decreased anxiety symptoms. Incorporating a handful of nuts or seeds into your daily diet can help you stay calm in stressful situations.

In short, eating a nutrient-rich diet provides your brain with the tools it needs to function optimally. Essential vitamins and minerals, such as B-complex vitamins and magnesium, play a crucial role in producing neurotransmitters such as serotonin and dopamine, which regulate mood and stress.

Probiotics

In addition, a balanced diet helps maintain a healthy gut microbiome, which in turn influences your mental health. The gut-brain axis is a bidirectional pathway where the state of your gut directly affects your mind.

A study published in *Trends in Neurosciences* by Foster and Neufeld (2013) highlights how a balanced gut microbiota reduces anxiety symptoms. Fermented foods such as yogurt, kimchi and kefir are excellent for promoting healthy gut flora and, thus, a calmer mind.

A wealth of evidence points to a strong connection between BDNF levels and the gut microbiome, the collection of microorganisms that live in the human digestive tract. Probiotics help you have a healthy microbiome, boosting cognitive function.

When people diagnosed with mild cognitive impairment took 800 milligrams of a Lactobacillus *plantarum* probiotic supplement for 12 weeks, they experienced rapid improvements in attention and memory. The greatest improvements in cognitive function in people taking the probiotic occurred in those with the greatest increases in serum BDNF levels, as expected.

So next time you plan your meals, incorporate more fruits, vegetables, whole grains, fish and nuts into your diet. These foods will not only nourish you physically but also strengthen your mental health.

Hydration

Another important aspect of your diet to keep in mind is maintaining good hydration by drinking enough water throughout the day, as dehydration negatively affects mood and increases anxiety. If you don't like the taste of plain water, you can add slices of lemon, lime or cucumber to give it a refreshing and natural touch. Staying hydrated will not only benefit your physical health but also your emotional and mental well-being.

Avoid the Use of Drugs and Alcohol

Finally, you should limit Alcohol and Drugs. They make you feel a momentary calm only to be sucked into a whirlwind of anxiety and stress later.

That's what alcohol and drugs do to your central nervous system, altering your brain chemistry and causing sudden mood swings. While they may initially offer a sense of relaxation, long-term abuse of these substances only aggravates anxiety, especially when you abstain from them.

They also interfere with your sleep, resulting in poor-quality rest. And we know that poor sleep only intensifies stress and anxiety.

So limiting alcohol and drug use is not only common sense; it's essential to maintaining your mental health and combating anxiety. Make this habit a priority and discover how your mind and body become stronger every day.

Natural Supplements Against Anxiety and Stress

One way your body responds to stress and anxiety is by releasing the hormone cortisol from the adrenal glands, which are located on top of the kidneys. When you are constantly stressed, your body releases cortisol, which negatively affects your long-term health.

Elevated cortisol has been associated with increased susceptibility to infections, which means you could get sick more often if you have chronically high levels of this stress hormone.

In the long term, excess cortisol increases your chances of developing major cardiovascular and metabolic diseases, such as type 2 diabetes, obesity, high blood pressure and heart disease. These health problems can significantly impact your quality of life and longevity.

Fortunately, researchers have identified some natural and safe ways to regulate cortisol levels and anxiety.

Specific plant extracts that have been clinically shown to safely reduce elevated cortisol and feelings of anxiety and stress have been identified.

Incorporating these plant extracts into your daily routine through supplements or herbal teas is an effective and safe way to modulate your stress response.

Lychee and Green Tea Blend

Lychee is an abundant fruit found throughout East Asia. It is consumed both as a fruit and for medicinal purposes.

Lychee is rich in polyphenols, compounds you've probably heard mentioned for their important role in certain biological activities. They are especially effective in reducing inflammation, fighting oxidative stress and preventing cell damage in the body.

Most lychee products you can find today contain long-chain polyphenols, which, unfortunately, are not easily absorbed in your intestinal tract. But don't worry because when combined with green tea, the lychee-green tea blend gives you a much more bioavailable extract than ordinary lychee extract, which means your body makes better use of it.

It has been found that the polyphenol content measured in the blood after using this blend was three times higher than after using just the lychee extract. Imagine the positive impact this can have on your health.

Two groups were created in a study conducted with young, healthy men. Participants in one group were assigned to take 100 mg of the lychee-green tea mixture daily, and those in the other group were assigned to take a placebo daily. After four weeks, those who received the mixture of extracts had very significant reductions in blood cortisol levels compared to those who did not receive it, as well as in the inflammatory cytokines IL-1beta and IL-6.

In another trial, 100 mg of the lychee-green tea mixture was administered twice daily to 10 healthy individuals for 10 days, followed by exercise under low-oxygenation conditions, to induce stress. The researchers found that the rate at which cortisol and inflammatory markers increased was significantly slower among subjects receiving the extracts than among individuals receiving the placebo. This demonstrates the power of this combination to help manage stress.

Magnolia and Phellodendron Bark

Two tree bark extracts have also been shown to reduce cortisol levels.

For centuries, the bark of the *Magnolia officinalis* tree, which grows at high altitudes in East Asia, has been used to combat various conditions, including anxiety, depression and stress. If you are looking for a natural way to reduce your stress level and improve your emotional well-being, this bark is also an excellent choice.

Another extract that has shown similar benefits is the bark of the *Phellodendron amurense* tree, which is used in traditional Chinese medicine. Animal studies have revealed that this extract reduces the biological markers of stress.

Imagine the power of combining these two bark extracts. That's exactly what researchers did in a recent study. They administered 250 mg of a mixture of Magnolia and Phellodendron bark extract or a placebo twice daily to people with moderate to high-stress levels. After four weeks, the results were impressive: only those taking the bark extracts experienced significant reductions in cortisol levels and stress.

Premenopausal, overweight women aged 20–50 years who suffered from consistently high levels of anxiety reported a significant decrease in anxiety symptoms after six weeks of taking these bark extracts.

The anti-anxiety benefits of Magnolia bark extract go beyond cortisol. The compounds found in *Magnolia officinalis* interact with certain receptors in the brain in a way that benefits your mood and psychological state.

You've heard in previous chapters about serotonin, sometimes dubbed the "happy hormone." This chemical is key to regulating stress, depression and mood. What you may not have known is that magnolia helps you increase your serotonin levels, as laboratory studies have shown. This means that incorporating magnolia extract into your routine could give you that extra boost of positivity you need.

Zinc

Zinc is the most abundant trace mineral in the brain. It influences BDNF expression and activity by stimulating proteins involved in converting biologically inactive BDNF (pro-BDNF) into mature BDNF. The RDA for adult men is 11 milligrams per day and 8 milligrams per day for adult women. Approximately 12% of adults in the United States do not get enough zinc in their diet, and up to 20% of older adults are deficient as well.

In a meta-analysis of multiple studies where participants received 30 milligrams of supplemental zinc daily for three months, zinc supplementation improved circulating BDNF levels better than a placebo. It is not the purpose of this book to go in-depth into the different types of diets but to give you the guidelines to do your research so that you can incorporate the one that best suits you, always keeping in mind the general indications of a healthy diet.

Other aspects related to diet are important for your mental health. Therefore, and in order not to duplicate the content, I invite you to look at the chapter that talks about the brain-derived neurotrophic factor, how diet can increase its production and its benefits. In the following pages, we will also detail another aspect, certainly related to food, which deserves a separate chapter: fasting.

Take control of your mental health through nutrition and discover the power of food to transform your life!

CHAPTER 10

Fasting: The Finest of Nature's Surgeries

"But when you fast, put oil on your head and wash your face, so that it will not be obvious to others that you are fasting, but only to your father, who is unseen; and your Father, who sees what is done in secret, will reward you."

Mateo 6:17-18

THE MAJESTIC MOUNTAIN SCENERY of the Sierra de Gredos, with its rugged peaks, green valleys and crystal-clear rivers, offered a perfect setting for disconnection and introspection. The center's facilities included cozy stone and wood cabins, perfectly integrated into the natural surroundings.

The retreat began in silence, with a serene welcome from the organizers. Marta and the other participants received instructions on preparing their bodies and minds for the fast. The first stage consisted of a light diet of fruits and vegetables, allowing the body to adapt gradually.

The first few days were a gentle adjustment. Martha became accustomed to simple meals and spent her hours exploring the quiet forest trails surrounding the retreat center. The fresh air and calm of the natural surroundings were already beginning to calm her mind, which was normally agitated by the constant hustle and bustle of the city.

On the third day, Martha began fasting, drinking water and resting. She felt nervous, unsure how her body would react to the lack of food. However, the tranquility of the place and the constant guidance of the facilitators helped her calm down. She spent the days walking the forest trails, meditating by the river and writing in her journal.

The first day was the most difficult. Her stomach grew, and her mind couldn't stop thinking about food. But as the hours passed, Martha began to notice something surprising. Her mind, usually crowded with uncontrolled thoughts, was clearing.

By the fourth day, Marta felt lighter, not only physically but mentally as well. A sense of peace and clarity began to settle inside her. Without the constant chore of digestion, her body had more energy for internal healing processes. She began to notice a deeper connection with her surroundings, with the trees, the birds and the wind rustling through the leaves and bushes.

On the sixth day, Martha experienced a revelation. Sitting by the river, with the sound of the water running gently between the rocks, she realized that the anxiety that had plagued her for years was not just caused by work or external expectations but by a disconnection from herself. The fast had acted as a mirror, reflecting her true needs and desires.

At the end of the retreat, Martha broke the fast with a light soup, savoring each bite with renewed gratitude. She returned to her daily life with a new perspective. She learned to incorporate periods of intermittent fasting into her routine as a health practice and as a ritual of reconnecting with herself.

Marta's story shows how fasting, beyond being a simple abstinence from food, can be a powerful tool for introspection and healing. Marta found the clarity and peace she so desperately sought in the silence and stillness.

***

There is an essential tool for preserving health and developing inner faculties: therapeutic and spiritual fasting.Your physical and spiritual bodies are vibratory extremes of the same essence: you. Your physical body, tangible and material, is spirit in its most condensed form, while your spirit is matter in its most sublime and ethereal state.

To understand this, think of how water can be liquid, solid as ice, and gaseous as vapor, changing its state without ceasing to be essentially water. So are you: a single energy manifesting in different ways. Your material body and your spirit are different states of the same energy.

In the same way that increasing luminosity reduces darkness or increasing heat reduces cold, depriving your physical body of essential nutrients weakens it. The other extreme, that is, the more subtle and spiritual in you, is strengthened.

That is why, after fasting for several days, your thoughts begin to have the clarity they lacked before. Your mind begins to see things from another perspective, higher, less conditioned by matter and closer to those dimensions that you only fully cross when you die and detach from the physical vehicle.

A quantum leap occurs in your consciousness, whereby the insight and speed of your intuitive mind, your right cerebral hemisphere, permeates your reasoning mind, your left cerebral hemisphere. You begin to experience amazing mental clarity, where thoughts easily flow and brilliant ideas arise spontaneously. The result is a certain degree of enlightenment or satori, an awakening to a deeper, transcendent reality. You feel as if a veil has been lifted, revealing hidden truths and allowing you to see the world with new eyes.

Fasting can be a memorable experience for you when you engage in creative activities, such as writing or painting, as inspiration knocks at your door with unusual force. You can almost touch it, feeling it vibrating in every fiber of your being. You are invaded by an electrifying energy that awakens all your senses and empowers your creative capacity to extraordinary levels. Ideas flow effortlessly, words dance on paper, and colors come alive on canvas.

Strolling through nature or watching a sunset become unforgettable events because of the special perception of colors and sensations. Every detail seems to take on a life of its own.

Doing a meditation after several days of fasting cannot be explained with words, and I encourage you to experience it since only in this way will you be able to see the before and after. It is an inner journey that transcends the physical and connects you with the very essence of your being and the quantum universe. You will feel how the barriers of your mind dissolve, and the mental clarity and inner peace you will experience will be so profound that it will permanently transform your perception of reality.

But let's get down to business. First of all, what is fasting?

Fasting is the voluntary abstention from ingesting solid food and liquids for a set period of time. When you fast, you give your digestive system a break and allow your body to focus on other important biological processes, such as detoxification and cell regeneration.

There is nothing better than examining how words are used to get a clear idea of their meaning. Every morning, upon waking up and having enjoyed a good night's rest, most people eat food in different forms and quantities, depending on their country and customs. This act is called "breakfast."

From a linguistic perspective, the word 'breakfast' means 'to break the fast,' referring to the period between dinner and the first meal of the day during which no food is consumed. This is the true meaning of fasting: the total, not partial, absence of food for a certain period of time.

I want to emphasize this concept since, nowadays, some types of mono dieting have become fashionable and are erroneously called fasting. During fasting, drinking water is allowed, not to be confused with drinking food in liquid form, such as fruit juices or syrups. The key is to stop the digestion process, and this acts whenever there is food to digest, even if the amounts are minimal. Also, I want to say that there is a type of fasting in which water intake is suspended, the so-called dry fasting, but it will not be analyzed here.

Why do human beings need to fast?

Let me use a simile familiar to everyone. The oil in your car has the mission to grease, lubricate and keep the engine in perfect condition. However, when the oil molecules come into contact with oxygen, they begin to oxidize, and over time, their function degrades until they finally break down. This means that it can no longer perform its function of lubricating, with the danger that this entails for the engine, which is why it must be changed from time to time. It is important to point out that when you change the oil in your car, the first thing you do is empty all the used oil, and it is not until the reservoir has been emptied and cleaned that the new oil is poured in. With the human body, something similar happens; there is a process of oxidation and degradation.

Today, the dominant paradigm in global health is the Western model. In the West, the emphasis is on the physical and on the intake of nutrients (yang principle) in the form of proteins, carbohydrates, vitamins and mineral salts. In other words, it recognizes that you have to change the oil in your body, just as you would your car, but neglects the importance of internal cleansing.

On the other hand, the Eastern model works on the more subtle energies, focusing on eliminating toxins and purifying the body (yin principle). In other words, it acknowledges that the old oil must be emptied before replacing it with new oil. This approach seeks to restore the body's natural balance, allowing the systems to function optimally and harmoniously.

By combining the health principles of both Western and Eastern yang and yin systems, you can take holistic care of your health, properly nourishing and ridding it of harmful residues that accumulate over time.

In short, if you want to get the most out of the nutrients in your diet, you must first cleanse your body of the debris generated by the eating process.

Reflect on this universal truth, as simple as all the great truths: Is it conceivable to fill your lungs with pure air without first expelling the stale air inside? What good would it do to fill a glass of liquid without first emptying it? These examples clearly illustrate the importance of emptying before filling and detoxifying your body before nourishing it. By following this principle, you will be in harmony with natural laws and will be able to reach an optimal state of health and well-being.

Animals and children use fasting instinctively to heal their organs when imbalanced. The wise nature makes it so that in certain situations, the appetite is lost, reacting to this even with vomiting, and it is only human stupidity that insists on giving food based on its established cultural-brain program.

Fasting was already used as a therapeutic method for spiritual growth by the oldest civilization of mankind, the Sumerian, from which its use spread to other peoples and cultures. Aristotle and Plato regularly practiced fasting to improve their physical and mental performance. Pythagoras fasted for 40 days and recommended its practice in his school of mysteries. The Bible contains dozens of allusions to prolonged fasting by Jesus and the apostles, as well as in the Mahabharata and the Upanishad, among many other ancient writings.

Hippocrates, the father of medicine in the 5th century B.C., said: *"Food in convalescence strengthens; in sickness, it weakens."*

What Biological Processes Take Place During a Fast?

During fasting, the body undergoes a series of metabolic changes. These changes trigger the expression of certain dormant genes, which in turn generates a cascade of positive effects, both physically and mentally. As the body adapts to the absence of food, alternative metabolic pathways are activated that promote cellular repair, hormone regulation and optimization of various physiological functions.

During the first phase of fasting, your body consumes glucose circulating in your blood and glycogen stored in your liver and muscles. This initial stage generally lasts between 24 and 48 hours, depending on your previous glycogen stores and your level of physical activity.

After this initial stage, you enter a state of deficiency or hypoglycemia. Although your body self-balances and your blood glucose normalizes later, you may experience mild, transient symptoms such as dizziness and cold sweats. Don't worry; these are normal signs of your body adapting to fasting.

During this second phase, internal mechanisms for consuming accumulated fat are set in motion. These processes act on the nerve endings, hypothalamus, adrenal glands and pancreas. The hypothalamus begins to release growth hormones, among other regulatory substances. At the same time, the pancreas decreases its insulin production to promote fat burning as an alternative energy source.

Thus, during fasting, your body will use mainly fat as fuel and occasionally non-essential proteins for life. These proteins, through a process called glycogenesis, will serve to gradually adapt your brain until it can use ketone bodies as its primary source of energy.

Once all the fat in the body is consumed, it will begin to consume the essential proteins for life, so at that point, the appetite returns, and you must eat. Otherwise, death will ensue.

Fasting triggers a series of physiological changes in the body that directly impact your physical and mental health.

Fasting helps regulate stress hormones, particularly cortisol, which makes you feel calmer and calmer.

Another wonder of fasting is its ability to reduce inflammation in the body. And you should know that chronic inflammation has been linked to several mental health disorders, including anxiety.

But its benefits don't end there. Researchers have found that fasting increases the production of BDNF, a pathway known to promote neuroplasticity and brain health.

In April 2022, an article entitled "Intermittent fasting and cognition: BDNF as a strategy to optimize brain health" was published in the scientific journal *Frontiers in Neuroendocrinology.* The research concluded that Intermittent Fasting elevated BDNF levels, leading to upregulation of protein synthesis.

In short, fasting is a tool for physical health and a powerful ally in anxiety management. Fasting offers a natural and effective relief by balancing stress hormones, providing a more stable energy source, reducing inflammation and increasing neuroplasticity.

There are different modalities of fasting, some of which are very fashionable nowadays. One such modality is intermittent fasting, which, in its most effective form, involves eating once a day and allowing the digestive system to rest for almost 24 hours.

If you are interested in using this tool, which, it must be said, is not for everyone, consult with your doctor or a specialized nutritionist to determine if fasting is right for you and, if so, what type of fasting is best suited to your needs and lifestyle.

With proper supervision and guidance, you can incorporate this ancient practice safely and effectively, taking advantage of its many benefits to your physical and mental well-being, including reducing anxiety and controlling recurring negative thoughts.

If you decide that fasting is not for you, don't worry. You can always explore the many other effective tools and techniques described throughout this book. You're sure to find some that you're more comfortable with and that best suit your unique lifestyle and personality.

CHAPTER 11
Sauna and Cold Baths

"Only the dose makes a thing not a poison."

Paracelso

SITTING ON THE SOIL *floor, Ana felt the sweat running down her skin. She breathed deeply, letting the heat and steam envelop her. All around her, the mud walls seemed to breathe with her, amplifying the sensation of being in a kind of earthly womb, a place of rebirth and purification.*

With a deep serenity in his eyes, a middle-aged man poured herbal-infused water over the red-hot volcanic stones in the center of the temazcal. The hiss of rising steam filled the space, mingling with the soft, rhythmic chanting that echoed in an ancient language. Ana closed her eyes, letting herself be carried away by the sound.

The warmth enveloped her body, penetrating her bones. Each breath brought with it the scent of herbs, providing a sense of cleansing and renewal. Ana could feel the tension built up in her body slowly fading away as if the sweat running down her skin was taking all her worries with it.

The outside world seemed far away. Only heat, steam and chanting existed in that small, dark space. Ana remembered her grandmother's words about the importance of the temazcal, not only as an ancestral tradition but also as a powerful healing rite for the body and soul. She felt a stronger connection to her roots and ancestors than ever.

Every drop of sweat that fell represented a release, a purging of the tensions that had plagued her in the city. The heat and steam purified her body and her mind, clearing away negative thoughts and filling her with a deep, revitalizing peace.

As the ceremony ended, the shaman opened the blanket covering the entrance, allowing the cool forest air to enter and caress her sweaty skin. Ana emerged outside, feeling light, as if she had left an immense burden inside the temazcal. The blue sky and the sounds of the forest seemed more vivid and clear than ever.

Ana knew she had found something very valuable in this experience. With a renewed sense of peace and healing, she was ready to face life with a new perspective. She knew she could always return to the temazcal, to that place of warmth, steam and chanting, whenever anxiety threatened to take hold again.

***

Have you ever wondered what happens to your body when you enter a hot environment like a temazcal or sauna? The science behind the benefits is truly fascinating. The moment your skin feels the scorching heat, a special circuit in the pre-optic area of your brain is activated, triggering a cascade of responses in your autonomic nervous system, including vasodilation of your blood vessels. The result? Blood flow throughout your body increases dramatically; the plasma volume in your bloodstream rises, and the systolic volume—that is, the amount of blood your heart pumps with each beat—also increases significantly. In fact, your heart rate can accelerate to between 100 and 150 beats per minute, similar to what you might experience during a cardio workout.

This set of effects closely resembles cardiovascular exercise. It's like cardio-vascular exercise but without the physical effort of mobilizing joints and limbs. Plus, it offers additional benefits, such as improvements in bone density.

Your vascular system adjusts to accommodate the increases in heart rate and blood volume. Essentially, you're getting a cardiovascular workout in that hot environment, even if you're just sitting.

Scientists at the University of Eastern Finland have spent the last few years researching the health benefits of their most renowned national pastime: sauna bathing.

And they have found many. Among them, sauna use is associated with a much lower risk of cardiovascular disease, Alzheimer's and other dementias, about 60% to 66% lower, if people use the sauna four to seven times a week. Therefore, sauna sessions appear to be very helpful in reducing the risk factors that contribute to cardiovascular disease.

As you know, good cardiovascular health also improves blood flow to the brain, which helps protect against dementia and other brain diseases.

There is also some molecular evidence for sauna use, and I'm very interested in heat shock proteins. What are heat shock proteins, and why do they matter to us? They are stress response proteins that help maintain the protein structure in cells, which is crucial for their function.

As we age, this ability to maintain protein structure deteriorates, and we now know that heat shock proteins help prevent proteins from becoming disorganized and unstructured, which can lead to plaque formation. There is a lot of evidence from animal studies showing that high levels of heat shock proteins protect against the formation of these plaques in the vascular system or in the brain, such as amyloid beta 42 plaques, which are associated with Alzheimer's disease.

Some studies have observed that people who sit in a sauna at about 80 degrees Celsius for 30 minutes activate their heat shock proteins by 50% over their baseline levels. Once activated, they remain elevated for about 48 hours. So, by using the sauna four to seven times a week, these proteins are likely to stay elevated constantly, helping to prevent plaque formation, among other things.

You may be surprised to learn that Dr. Rhonda Patrick conducted a fascinating experiment at the Salk Institute for Biological Studies. She injected fragments of amyloid beta 42 peptides into nematode worms, which caused them to suffer paralysis due to the formation of protein aggregates in their muscles. She then decided to increase their heat shock proteins, and to her surprise, she observed that these worms could move again despite the injection of amyloid beta 42. This discovery suggests that activating heat shock proteins could be a powerful strategy to combat the negative effects of harmful protein accumulation in the human body.

And you may be wondering, do sauna baths have a direct effect on anxiety and stress?

I'm going to tell you about a couple of fascinating studies. The first explored the hormonal changes in people who took sauna sessions, including the production of hormones from the adrenal glands, the testicles, and even the brain.

The study, titled *"Endocrine effects of heat stress and cold water immersion in young adult men,"* conducted in 2021, involved men who attended four Finnish sauna sessions of 12 minutes each. The sauna temperature was 90 to 91 degrees Celsius. They then had a six-minute break in cold water of about 10 degrees Celsius. Hormones, including testosterone, DHEA, prolactin, and cortisol, were measured before, during, and after the study. The main finding was a significant decrease in cortisol production. This means that the sauna sessions effectively reduced the stress hormone levels in their body.

Repeated exposure to intense heat followed by cold immersions modulates the endocrine system, helping regulate the body's response to stressful situations. The 12-minute protocol in a 90-degree environment, followed by a six-minute cool-down in cold water, showed a marked reduction in cortisol levels.

This is especially interesting because many people suffer from acute and chronic stress, and controlling cortisol is a challenge. Imagine being able to reduce your levels of this stress hormone in a way as simple and natural as enjoying a sauna followed by a dip in cold water. Sounds almost too good to be true, doesn't it? Science backs up that these extreme temperature changes help your body better regulate its response to stressful situations. So, the next time you feel stress creeping up on you, consider trying this thermal contrast technique to calm your system and bring it back into balance.

The second is a study conducted on 34 healthy males, published in the Journal of Thermal Biology in 2020. The title is *"Repeated exposure to hyperthermia increases circulating Brain-Derived Neurotrophic Factor levels, which is associated with improved quality of life and reduced anxiety: a randomized controlled trial."*

The study concludes that regular sauna sessions can significantly raise one's BDNF (Brain-Derived Neurotrophic Factor) levels, even more than moderate exercise.

Why Should You Be Interested in Raising Your BDNF Levels?

BDNF increases neurogenesis and neuroplasticity in your brain. Neurogenesis is the fascinating ability of your brain to create new neurons throughout your life. Neuroplasticity, on the other hand, is the amazing ability of your brain to adapt and reorganize itself in response to the environmental stimuli you experience.

By increasing the presence of this protein in your body, you will improve the health of your brain, reduce your anxiety levels and reduce your risk of suffering from neurodegenerative diseases in the future.

In addition, exposure to the sauna's heat causes mild, controlled stress. This stress stimulates the production of norepinephrine and prolactin, helping the body regulate its stress response in everyday situations.

In addition, prolactin supports the production and repair of myelin in the nervous system. Myelin is the substance we discussed that coats and protects nerve fibers. It is crucial for the fast and efficient conduction of nerve impulses in the body.

So here's an effective tool for managing stress. It's not completely free, as you need access to hot and cold water, but the benefits can be enormous. This simple method can offer significant stress relief and help you maintain the right hormonal balance in your body. Why not give it a try and see how you feel?

Tool: Sauna and Cold Baths

To maximize the benefits of sauna use, here are the essential guidelines for a healthy person:

First, limit your sauna sessions to a maximum of 20 minutes and rest between sessions. This will allow you to experience the positive effects without overtaxing your body. Remember to listen to your body and leave early if you feel uncomfortable or dizzy.

Also, be sure to hydrate properly before and after each session. Drink plenty of cool water to replace fluids lost through sweating. Avoid alcoholic or caffeinated beverages, as they can further dehydrate you.

Try to enjoy the sauna 4 to 5 times a week for the greatest benefits. Studies show that this frequency will allow you to consistently experience positive effects on your health and well-being. Incorporate sauna sessions into your weekly routine as part of your self-care and relaxation time. Remember, consistency is key to seeing lasting results. So make a commitment to yourself and prioritize these sauna moments regularly. Your body and mind will thank you.

The minimum recommended temperature is 78.9°C, ideally between 80°C and 90°C. Adjust the temperature within this range to get the maximum benefits without overheating your body. If you are new to sauna use, start with lower temperatures and gradually increase as you become more comfortable. Listen to your body and get out of the sauna if you feel any discomfort or dizziness.

You can alternate heat with cold water baths for even more benefits. Studies show that with as little as 11 minutes a week of immersion in cold water baths, your body experiences significant positive effects.

The information provided here is intended to educate and should not be used as a substitute for professional medical advice, diagnosis or treatment. If you are pregnant, have a chronic illness or any medical condition, it is crucial that you consult your physician before beginning any sauna regimen.

CHAPTER 12
Massage

"Massage not only touches the body, but also the soul. It is a bridge to the serenity and inner peace that we all seek."

Anonymous

UPON ARRIVING AT THE center, Manuel was greeted by Ana, a therapist, who had a warm smile and a calming energy. Ana led him into a brightly lit room with soft lights and soothing music playing in the background. Manuel lay down on the massage table, feeling a hint of relief for the first time in a long time.

Ana began with gentle, firm strokes, working Manuel's tense muscles. "Massage is known for its ability to relax the body and mind," Ana explained as she continued her work.

Manuel noticed a change as Ana's expert hands unraveled knots and tensions. His breathing deepened and slowed, his mind stopped racing, and, for a moment, he felt a peace that had eluded him for so long.

After several sessions, Manuel began to notice deeper changes in his life. Mornings were no longer a mental battleground, and the load on his shoulders felt lighter. The tension, which had been his constant companion, began to fade.

One day, Manuel realized something important while having coffee with his best friend. "I don't know how to explain it," he said, "but I feel like I'm regaining control of my life. The massage has been a revelation. Not only does it relax me in the moment, but it has taught me to live more calmly."

Intrigued, his friend decided to research the benefits of massage. He discovered clinical studies, such as one published in the Journal of Clinical Psychiatry, that confirmed what Manuel had experienced. Patients with Generalized Anxiety Disorder who received Swedish massage showed a significant reduction in their anxiety levels, with lasting effects beyond the treatment.

Manuel became a staunch advocate of therapeutic massage, sharing his story and encouraging others to try it. At every opportunity, he recalled Ana's words, "Massage is more than a luxury; it is a powerful tool for healing the body and mind."

***

In the groundbreaking study Manuel's friend found, published in the "Journal of Clinical Psychiatry," scientists discovered that Swedish massage was a powerful tool for reducing anxiety. Sixty-eight people diagnosed with generalized anxiety disorder (GAD) participated, a group that is well aware of the havoc that anxiety can wreak.

The participants were divided into two groups: one received regular Swedish massage, and the other received no treatment. Those fortunate enough to receive massage enjoyed one-hour sessions twice a week for three months. At the end of the study, if you had been one of those who received massage, you would have seen your anxiety levels decrease by a staggering 40%.

This transformation was not just temporary. The benefits of massage were maintained even six weeks after the sessions ended, providing not only immediate relief but also a long-term reduction in anxiety.

In other eye-opening research published in the Journal of Alternative and Complementary Medicine, scientists investigated how massage alters your body chemistry to improve your mood and reduce anxiety and depression.

Fifty people with anxiety and depression joined this fascinating study. They received therapeutic massage sessions for a full hour once a week for two months at a time.

At the end of the period, cortisol levels, the stress hormone, were found to have decreased significantly in all participants. There was also an increase in serotonin and dopamine levels, the chemicals in the brain that improve your mood and make you feel good.

Participants, in their testimonials, reported feeling less anxiety and depression and an overall improvement in their mood and well-being.

These studies open the door to a new approach to the treatment of anxiety. We are not talking about drugs with side effects or temporary solutions. We're discussing a natural, effective, enjoyable treatment that can change your life. Imagine being able to free yourself from those uncontrolled thoughts and anxiety that overwhelm you and replace them with a sense of calm and well-being. Imagine facing each day with renewed energy and optimism without anxiety holding you back. That's what therapeutic massage can do for you.

In short, therapeutic massage is a powerful tool that works on multiple levels to reduce stress and anxiety.

Massage activates your parasympathetic nervous system, whose main function is to allow a state of relaxation or rest. This system is the natural antidote to the "fight or flight" response that stress triggers in your body through the sympathetic system. Your body begins to release a cascade of neurotransmitters such as serotonin and dopamine. These natural chemicals are known for their calming and mood-enhancing effects. In addition, massage reduces cortisol levels, the stress hormone, providing deep and lasting relief.

When you receive a therapeutic massage, your body enters a state of deep relaxation where tension dissipates, your heart rate slows, and your blood pressure decreases. Massage is like a switch that turns off your survival mode and turns on your relaxation mode.

Massage Tool

Discover the transformative power of touch and allow your body and mind to relax and rejuvenate! Treat yourself to a massage every now and then!

CHAPTER 13
Proper Rest

"Sleep is the best meditation."

Dalai Lama

ONCE UPON A TIME, *in Silicon Valley, there was a computer named Orion. Orion was no ordinary computer; it was the fastest, most efficient and brightest in town. Its owner, a programmer named Alex, relied on it for everything from writing code to storing digital memories. Orion was the tireless hero of all daily tasks.*

In the beginning, everything was perfect. Orion processed data at the speed of light, solved complex problems and never failed to keep Alex up to date with his projects. However, there was one small problem: Orion never shut down. Day and night, Orion's circuits worked, lights flickered, and fans spun incessantly. While other computers took their well-deserved breaks, Orion worked without pause.

At first, Orion was proud of its ability to run continuously. But over time, he began to notice that something wasn't right. His fans started making strange noises, the circuits were heating up faster, and the screens were displaying errors more frequently. Orion tried to ignore these problems, determined not to disappoint Alex.

One night, while Alex slept, Orion tried compiling a huge program. The code was complex and unwieldy. Orion felt his components overloaded, but he kept going. Suddenly, in the middle of a line of code, Orion froze. His blue screen, the dreaded "screen of death," appeared. For the first time, Orion was forced to stop.

Alex woke up alarmed by the sound of the crazed fan. He ran over to Orion and saw the blue screen. "It can't be," Alex thought, "Orion never fails." He tried rebooting it several times, but each attempt was futile. Orion was crashing.

Desperate, Alex took Orion to a technician named Thomas, known to be the best at hardware and software repairs. Thomas examined Orion closely and then looked at Alex. "Your computer is exhausted," Thomas said. "You never turn it off, do you? It needs rest, just like you do."

Alex was stunned. He had never thought that a computer or machine could need rest. Thomas explained that electronic components, though efficient, need breaks to cool down and recover. "Without rest, systems overload, fail and eventually break down," he added.

Thomas worked for hours, cleaning, repairing and optimizing Orion. Finally, he rebooted it and shut down the system completely for the first time in a long time. "Let it rest tonight," he told Alex. "Tomorrow, he'll be good as new."

The next day, Orion powered up without a hitch and ran better than ever. Alex decided to establish a new routine for Orion: he would give it breaks.

Orion was back to his usual efficient and brilliant computer. The lesson was clear: even the most efficient machines need rest to perform at their best. And so both Orion and Alex lived and worked better, always remembering the importance of a good rest.

***

Your brain is like a computer. When you don't get enough sleep, it's as if that computer is running non-stop without any rest. What happens then? It slows down, heats up and eventually starts to crash. Processes become slower, tasks take longer to complete, and the quality of work decreases. Mistakes you wouldn't normally make start to show up. You feel exhausted, frustrated and unable to perform at your best.

Just as a computer needs time to cool down, your mind also needs rest. Sleep gives your brain a chance to recharge, and you wake up refreshed and ready to face new challenges.

Lack of sleep decreases one's ability to manage stress effectively. When one doesn't get enough sleep, the brain is in a state of overload, reducing its ability to process and handle stressful situations properly. This can lead to overreaction to circumstances that would not normally cause one so much stress. Suddenly, everyday situations such as traffic, work deadlines, or small conflicts become almost impossible.

This increased sensitivity to stress only aggravates your anxiety symptoms, trapping you in a negative spiral where stress and anxiety constantly feedback on each other. The more anxiety you feel, the harder it is to fall asleep, and the less sleep you get, the more vulnerable you are to stress. It's a vicious cycle that can be difficult to break.

Sleep deprivation affects the production of certain neurotransmitters, such as serotonin and dopamine, that you already know very well. These neurotransmitters you already know are crucial for mood and anxiety regulation.

Lack of sleep also raises your levels of cortisol, the stress hormone. Increased cortisol due to sleep deprivation can put you in a constant state of alertness and tension, increasing your feelings of anxiety.

When you suffer from lack of sleep, you are more prone to fall into obsessive thought patterns, that negative cycle of ideas that repeat over and over in your mind. You find yourself caught in a loop of constant worries that you can't stop. The more you obsess over those thoughts, the harder it becomes to escape from them and the more anxiety you generate. It's a vicious cycle that feeds back on itself, where lack of sleep and negative thoughts power each other, driving you into a state of constant mental anguish.

When you are sleep-deprived, your ability to evaluate situations objectively is seriously compromised. Problems that you would normally be able to handle with relative ease suddenly become insurmountable mountains in your mind. This distorted perception of reality only increases your anxiety levels, as you feel completely unable to handle even the most mundane situations effectively. You find yourself trapped in a state of constant worry and stress, where every small obstacle seems like an insurmountable challenge.

Irritability due to lack of sleep can lead to conflicts in your personal relationships. Your tendency to overreact to minor situations can cause friction with friends, family and co-workers. You may find yourself arguing over trivial things or feeling frustrated with the people around you, even when you know it's not their fault. Again, these conflicts only increase your anxiety levels, creating a stressful environment in both your home and workplace. You feel trapped in a cycle of negativity and tension, affecting your ability to fall asleep at night, perpetuating the problem.

In short, lack of rest not only has a significant impact on your physical health but also exacerbates anxiety symptoms.

Once we understand how important it is to get a good night's sleep, we will look at various strategies to improve sleep quality. We will explore healthy sleep routines, such as creating an environment conducive to rest, adopting relaxing habits before bedtime, and understanding the impact of diet on your sleep.

Your body has an internal clock called the circadian rhythm that regulates your sleep-wake cycle. If you have trouble falling asleep, you should know that keeping regular bedtime and wake-up times helps synchronize this internal clock. Waking up and going to bed at the same time every day, even on weekends, stabilizes your sleep cycle. This translates into less daytime sleepiness and improved mood and productivity. To implement this routine, start by setting a bedtime that allows you to sleep between 7 and 9 hours. Adjust your schedule gradually until you reach your goal.

Your bedroom should be a sanctuary for rest. The right environment can do wonders for your sleep, so be sure to create optimal conditions. Keep your bedroom cool, between 15 and 20 degrees Celsius. It should not be too hot or cold so your body can regulate its temperature naturally.

Darkness is your ally when it comes to falling asleep, so use blackout curtains or a sleep mask and keep light to a minimum. Invest in a good mattress and pillows that conform to your body and give you the support you need.

A quiet environment is also conducive to sleep, so if you can't avoid external noise, consider using earplugs. With these simple adjustments, you'll turn your bedroom into an oasis of calm that invites you to sink into a restorative sleep each night.

You should avoid using electronic devices such as smartphones, tablets, computers and televisions at least one hour before bedtime. Did you know that blue light from screens can rob you of sleep? That's right. Blue light tricks your brain into thinking it's still daytime and suppresses the production of melatonin, the sleep hormone. This delays the onset of sleep and makes it difficult for you to relax and fall asleep.

Instead, opt for relaxing activities that help you unwind, such as reading a book under a dim light and letting yourself drift off into the pages of a captivating story. Soak in a warm bath before bed, allowing the warm water to soothe your tense muscles and calm your mind. Listen to relaxing music.

These activities will help prepare you for deep, rejuvenating sleep, chasing away the day's worries and creating an environment conducive to rest.

What you eat and drink has a big impact on the quality of your sleep. Avoid heavy and abundant meals at least two hours before bedtime, as they can cause indigestion and make it difficult to fall asleep. Opt for easy-to-digest dinners that do not overload your digestive system.

Some foods are your allies, while others can be your enemies in the quest for restful sleep. Dairy products, such as warm milk or yogurt, contain tryptophan, an amino acid that helps produce melatonin and serotonin, which regulate your sleep cycle. Bananas, rich in magnesium and potassium, help you relax your muscles and calm your nervous system. Oatmeal, meanwhile, contains natural melatonin and complex carbohydrates that induce a feeling of drowsiness. Nuts and seeds, such as almonds and pumpkin seeds, are excellent sources of magnesium and melatonin, which can significantly improve the quality of your sleep.

On the other hand, there are foods you should avoid before bedtime. Spicy foods can cause indigestion and heartburn, making it difficult to rest. Caffeine and nicotine are stimulants that can significantly interfere with your ability to relax and sleep soundly. Avoid coffee, tea, caffeinated soft drinks and cigarettes several hours before bedtime. Although alcohol may initially induce drowsiness, it disrupts deeper, more restful sleep cycles, leaving you feeling tired upon awakening. Moderate your consumption, especially at night.

Chocolate and caffeine contain theobromine, a stimulant that can increase your heart rate and brain activity. To promote deep sleep, be aware of these foods and limit their consumption, especially in the hours before bedtime.

In the quest for restful sleep, you may need extra help. Dietary supplements can be an effective option to improve the quality of your sleep.

I do not recommend taking melatonin, although it is the hormone that regulates sleep and is one of the most popular choices. The reason is that when you ingest this hormone externally, your body stops producing it internally. In the long run, this can upset your natural hormonal balance and create a dependency. You should stimulate the natural production of melatonin in your body. This is achieved by adapting to circadian rhythms: make sure you sleep at night in absolute darkness, with no lights or electronic devices on, and during the day, expose yourself to natural sunlight whenever you can and avoid wearing sunglasses, as they block some of that beneficial light. Let your body regulate itself naturally by following the cycles of light and dark. This way, you can gradually restore your internal melatonin production naturally.

One supplement you might consider is **valerian**. This medicinal herb has been used for centuries to treat insomnia and anxiety. Valerian can help you relax, reduce tension and shorten the time it takes to fall asleep. Also, unlike other sedatives, valerian does not cause dependence or side effects in most people. Between 300 and 600 mg of valerian extract, taken 30 minutes to two hours before bedtime.

Passionflower is another herb known for its calming properties. It can reduce anxiety and promote sleep by increasing brain levels of GABA, a neurotransmitter that induces a state of relaxation.

To reap the benefits of passionflower, it is suggested to take between 300 and 600 mg of standardized extract, ideally 30 minutes to an hour before bedtime. This will give you enough time for the active compounds to take effect and help you relax for a restful night's sleep.

Magnesium also plays an important role in sleep regulation. A deficit of this mineral can contribute to sleep problems. Magnesium helps calm the nervous system, relax muscles, and reduce stress and anxiety. Doses usually range from 200 to 400 mg daily, but remember to consult your doctor before taking any supplement to make sure it is right for you. Incorporating magnesium-rich foods into your diet, such as green leafy vegetables, nuts and seeds, is also beneficial for optimizing your levels of this important mineral.

Tryptophan is an essential amino acid that plays a crucial role in the production of serotonin, a neurotransmitter that helps regulate mood and sleep. It is found in foods such as turkey, chicken, eggs, dairy products, and nuts.

L-theanine is an amino acid found in **green tea** and is known for its calming effects without causing drowsiness. You can take L-theanine supplements or simply enjoy a cup of green tea to take advantage of its benefits. Between 100 and 200 mg, taken before bedtime.

In short, improving the quality of your sleep is simpler than it sounds. Adjust your daily routine, optimize your sleeping environment, adopt good habits before bedtime and take care of your diet. By doing so, you will improve your sleep and mental and emotional health, reducing anxiety and improving your overall well-being. You can change your life; start with a good night's sleep!

CHAPTER 14

Forest Bathing

"Nature is the art of God."

Dante

AMANECER WAS A YOUNG *girl of the Sioux tribe living on the vast plains of northern America. From a very young age, her grandmother had taught her to respect and revere Mother Nature, who provided everything necessary to live in harmony and health. Dawn's grandmother, Wise Elder, at nightly fires, would tell her stories about how Sioux ancestors connected deeply with the natural world to maintain a balance between body and spirit.*

One day, Dawn awoke feeling restless. She had been suffering from nightmares and a growing restlessness with no apparent cause that she could not understand. She remembered her grandmother's words: "When your spirit feels lost, return to the arms of Mother Nature. She will guide you back to peace."

Determined to follow the advice, Dawn went into the nearby forest. She walked barefoot on the damp earth, feeling every root and stone beneath her feet. The fresh, clean air filled her lungs as she listened to the birds singing. She sat by the river and closed her eyes, listening to the sound of the flowing water and calming her mind.

As the hours passed, Dawn began to feel more grounded. Once again, she evoked Wise Elder's teachings about the healing power of nature. *The Sioux believed that every tree, every stone and every animal had a spirit of its own, and by connecting with them, one could find balance and strength.*

She picked some sage leaves, a plant sacred to her people, and rubbed them between her hands, inhaling their soothing aroma. She lay back on the grass, looking up at the blue sky and feeling the warmth of the sun on her skin. Slowly, the thoughts that tormented her dissipated, replaced by a deep sense of peace.

Dawn spent the entire day in the forest. Returning to her village at dusk, she felt renewed, filled with a serenity she had not experienced in a long time. She knew Mother Nature had listened to and healed her, just as she had done with her ancestors.

***

Have you ever wondered why you feel so refreshed after a walk in the fresh air? The importance of fresh air and sunlight may seem like a no-brainer. However, beyond this intuition, there is a practice that takes these benefits to a higher level: *shinrin yoku* or forest bathing.

Shinrin yoku is a Japanese practice that involves spending time in the forest with a meditative and receptive attitude to improve health, well-being and happiness through contact with nature. In Japanese, "*Shinrin*" means "forest," while "*Yoku*" means "bathing." Although the term *shinrin yoku* is Japanese, the concept of harmonizing with nature to improve human health has been recognized by various cultures throughout history. This practice is a spiritual cure where "bathing" in the forest involves enjoying the environment while walking aimlessly to soak in the natural surroundings. This simple act of presence significantly reduces your stress levels.

Developed in Japan in the 1980s, *"shinrin yoku"* emerged as a response to protect the body against modern-day stress. The Japanese rediscovered that harmonizing with nature could provide remarkable relief from anxiety and depression.

Akasawa Shizen Kyuyourin, a national park in Nagano, is known as the place where this practice supposedly began.

In the 1990s, researchers studied the physiological benefits of forest bathing, providing scientific data that confirmed what we intuitively knew: spending time in nature is good for our health and immune system.

Later, a comprehensive study by Kotera, Richardson and Sheffield in 2022 showed that *shinrin yoku* has a remarkable impact on reducing anxiety symptoms. Participants experienced a significant decrease in symptoms related to anxiety disorders. It's as if the forest has the power to calm your restless mind.

But there's more. In 2023, Langer and his team conducted a pilot study with university students in the Valdivian Forest. The results were also surprising. After participating in forest bathing sessions, the young people showed a marked improvement in their anxiety levels.

And if you still need more proof, Dr. Kirsten McEwan and her team at the University of Derby found that people who practice *shinrin yoku* in forests experience a 29% reduction in their anxiety in just two hours. Can you believe it? In just 120 minutes, you can feel significantly calmer.

Can you imagine being able to relieve your anxiety naturally without resorting to medication? This study reveals that it is possible.

The connection between forest bathing and mental health is clear. Forest bathing participants have been found to have elevated levels of serotonin, a neurotransmitter associated with mood regulation and anxiety reduction.

The natural environment, filled with trees and plants, releases phytoncides, volatile organic compounds that plants emit to protect themselves from insects and disease. Inhaling these phytoncides positively influences serotonin regulation.

Additional studies have shown that natural sounds, such as birdsong, the murmur of the stream or the rustle of the wind through the trees, have a calming effect on the nervous system, helping to reduce levels of the stress hormone cortisol.

These studies used advanced technologies, such as electroencephalograms (EEGs), to measure brain activity. The electroencephalogram images of alpha and beta waves showed significant changes in the participants' brain activity during and after the forest baths.

Alpha waves are associated with relaxation and meditation, while beta waves are related to active thinking and problem-solving. The studies found that exposure to the forest environment increased alpha wave activity, indicating a state of deep relaxation and stress reduction.

The conclusion is clear. Spending time in nature is a powerful way to lower your anxiety levels.

You don't need to take long, frequent hikes through national parks to reap the benefits. There are practical alternatives you can incorporate into your daily life. A quick walk through the local park or spending time in a garden can have positive effects. The key is to connect with the natural environment.

Always remember that the path to a peaceful mind and healthy body does not require complicated solutions but simple and successful ones, so incorporate spending time in contact with nature into your schedule!

CHAPTER 15
Emotional-Mental Level

THE EMOTIONAL-MENTAL LEVEL OF the human being encompasses both emotions and thoughts. This level is crucial for facing life's challenges, making decisions, and maintaining healthy and satisfying relationships.

There is a deep interconnection between the way you think, feel and behave. Every thought you have is an interpretation of your experiences. When you cultivate positive, optimistic thoughts, you improve your overall well-being.

Conversely, when you immerse yourself in negative, pessimistic and catastrophic thoughts, you generate stress and anxiety. Your emotions also play a crucial role.

You can experience positive emotions that uplift you, such as joy, gratitude, enthusiasm and love. These emotions expand your mind and connect you to your best self.

But you can also feel negative emotions that depress you, such as fear, sadness, guilt and anger.

This interaction between thoughts and emotions is bidirectional. Your emotions color your perception and the way you think. And at the same time, your thoughts shape the emotions you feel. It is a constant cycle of mutual influence. Emotions and thoughts influence your behaviors. For example, confidence drives you to face new challenges, while insecurity leads you to avoid them.

Thinking that an event is dangerous generates fear while interpreting it as an opportunity generates enthusiasm. Likewise, emotions influence your thoughts. It is at this emotional-mental level where anxiety and stress develop, affecting your well-being and quality of life.

For this reason, although the tools you will see in the following chapters are very effective, it is advisable, as I have already said, to focus at first, especially if your anxiety level is very high, on the somatic tools of the physical-pranic level that indirectly affect the emotional-mental level.

The tools seen in the previous chapters will help you calm your body and vital energy, which will positively affect your emotions and thoughts. In this way, you will give rest to an emotional and mental level that is naturally overactive when you suffer from stress and anxiety, allowing you to gradually regain balance and inner calm.

However, as soon as you notice that your mind is calming down, you can and should add the new tools of the next chapters that will allow you to establish and strengthen adequate emotional and thinking habits.

CHAPTER 16

Art Therapy

"The purpose of art is to wash the dust of daily life off our souls."
Pablo Picasso

SOFIA FOUND HERSELF IN *her favorite spot in the park, a secluded corner near the pond, where the ducks swam with enviable calm. She closed her eyes and breathed deeply, trying to imitate the serenity of the water, but her mind was still filled with agitated thoughts and recurring fears.*

While surfing the Internet for answers, Sofia stumbled upon an article about art therapy one afternoon. She was intrigued by the idea of using art to calm her mind, so she decided to try it. The next day, she visited a nearby art store and bought a blank canvas, a set of brushes and a set of acrylic paints.

Back at home, Sofia arranged her new acquisitions on the dining room table, creating a small makeshift studio. She felt a mixture of excitement and nervousness as she prepared to begin. She picked up a paintbrush, dipped it in blue paint, and glided it across the canvas. At first, her movements were clumsy, reflecting her uncertainty. But little by little, she began to lose herself in the act of painting.

Each brushstroke seemed to relieve a little of the tension inside her. Sofia had no clear plan for what she wanted to create; she simply let her emotions guide her hands. The colors blended and flowed, forming abstract patterns that captured her inner state.

After an hour, she stopped to look at her work. It was not a perfect painting, nor was it intended to be. But in those chaotic strokes and vibrant coloring, she saw a reflection of her feelings, a tangible representation of her inner struggle. She felt a sense of relief for the first time in a long time.

That night, Sofia slept soundly without the usual invasion of thoughts. When she awoke, she decided to make painting a part of her daily routine. Every day, she spent an hour expressing herself through art, using the canvas as a safe space to release her emotions without judgment.

Over time, her paintings became more complex and nuanced. Sofia found that she was learning to manage her stress and better understand herself. The creative process allowed her to explore her feelings in a way that words could not.

She began to share her experience with friends and family, who were surprised to see how painting had transformed her. Some of them, inspired by her story, also began to experiment with art as a form of therapy.

Thus, Sofia found art therapy not only a tool to manage her anxiety but also a means to reconnect with her essence and discover new facets of herself.

***

In this chapter, you will discover how art therapy, especially painting, can be a powerful tool to manage anxiety. You will find out how to start your own healing journey through art.

The brain comprises billions of neurons connected by synapses, and these connections continually shift and strengthen or weaken based on your experiences. The brain is not a static organ; various environmental, behavioral and neural factors can modify its structure and function.

For this reason, artistic activity is incredibly therapeutic, as it has been shown to improve cognitive function and emotional well-being, as well as significantly reduce symptoms of anxiety and depression.

I'm going to show you how to use therapeutic art to manage your stress effectively. First, find a space where you feel comfortable and are not interrupted. Light a salt lamp, some candles, dim lights or even an essential oil diffuser to create a relaxing environment. You will need paper, cardboard, or canvas, as well as any drawing or painting materials.

Before you begin, set a clear intention: to make art to relieve stress without judging your work. Open yourself to the creative process without expectations.

Anxiety is that nagging feeling of excessive worry about things that, in reality, we shouldn't be so worried about. This worry is directly related to fear.

When you practice any form of artistic expression, you aim to interrupt and distract those overwhelming thoughts and emotions by focusing on a creative activity. By immersing yourself in the artistic process, you focus on the present—the tactile sensations of the materials and the exploration of colors, shapes, and textures. As you let yourself be carried away by the creative experience, your worries and anxieties recede into the background, giving you a respite and a safe space to express yourself.

Research on art therapy and anxiety has found impressive results: a significant reduction in anxiety symptoms and an increase in perceived quality of life. Best of all, these positive effects can last up to three months after art therapy sessions, which means that regular art practice can have a lasting impact on your mental and emotional well-being.

Here are some artistic expression activities you can do on your own to find immediate relief when anxiety creeps up on you:

Coloring books for adults: Coloring books are enjoyable for most people because they have clear boundaries. Immerse yourself in this relaxing activity that will help you unwind from your worries.

Create art with mandalas: Mandalas are composed of circular objects and designs that give a sense of control and tranquility. Working in circles has a rhythmic and calming effect. You can even draw your own circles without creating a complete mandala.

Painting: When you are completely determined to dive into art, you can, for very little money, buy the necessary materials that will certainly delight you: canvases, cardboard, paper and acrylic or other paints.

Art can be extremely therapeutic. Many studies prove this. Watching the colors blend and flow on the paper or canvas, especially with watercolor or acrylic, is especially beneficial and calming. This process allows you to disconnect your conscious mind and let your subconscious take control of the brush.

The First Exercise

I invite you to paint your emotions. It may sound a little strange at first, but it is similar to opening a journal and starting to write down how you feel. Instead of words, you will use colors and shapes.

You'll keep everything abstract to keep the conscious mind from intervening too much in the creative process. If you're experiencing a lot of anxiety right now, you might use zigzagging shapes and jagged lines to represent that feeling of inner restlessness. Or, if you are feeling angry about a recent situation, you could use intense shades of red and orange to express that pent-up anger.

Start by painting a background on the canvas or paper, gradually adding different shapes and strokes reflecting your feelings. Let your hand move freely without judging the final result. Remember that the goal is not to create a masterpiece but to allow you to explore and channel your inner world through art.

Use the colors that best represent your emotions at that moment. Don't worry about giving a specific meaning to each color; just let your mind choose, and don't overthink it. Allow yourself to explore different shades and combinations without judging whether they look "right" or "wrong." Trust your intuition and what each color conveys to you. You may be surprised to find that certain unexpected colors appear in your work, reflecting nuances of your emotional state that you had not consciously considered. This exercise is about freedom of expression, not technical perfection.

Allow the brush to move freely on the canvas. Perhaps your strokes are energetic and vibrant, with an intense color palette that screams the anxiety or stress you carry inside. Or maybe your painting is a haven of peace, with soft tones and gentle brushstrokes that evoke a state of calm and serenity.

Let the painting be your confidant, a mirror of your soul where you can be honest with yourself.

The Next Exercise

I recommend calming your mind in a similar way, but instead of painting your emotions, paint what represents peace to you. It can be a landscape that evokes a sense of deep tranquility and well-being. It may be the vastness of the ocean at sunrise. Or you may prefer to lose yourself in the serenity of a desert sunset, marveling at the palette of warm colors that tint the sky as the sun dips below the horizon. You may find peace by wandering into the thicket of an ancient forest surrounded by centuries-old trees. That special place is unique to you, an inner refuge you can go to whenever you need to reconnect with your inner peace.

Paint a very loose, colorful version of that place of peace. Don't worry about the details; just use broad brush strokes to capture the essence of that place. Let your subconscious guide the brush and express itself through the colors and movements. Don't seek perfection; seek inner peace. Let your mind free and flow with each stroke.

While painting, your goal is to turn off your conscious mind and let yourself be carried away by the act of creating. Allow yourself to immerse yourself in the sensory experience of the colors, textures and movements of the brush on the canvas. Don't worry about re-adding details or obsessing over any specific part of your painting.

Remember that this exercise is not about creating a masterpiece to show the world but about calming your mind. It is a therapeutic process, a form of meditation through art that will help you quiet your thoughts and connect with your purest essence.

Sometimes, it may seem that what we paint is not good, but that is not the important thing. What is crucial is that you flow and use your imagination and your subconscious to communicate through art. Instead of writing or telling yourself to calm down, you express the calmness you long for.

The Third Exercise

I propose a variation of the first. It was developed by the Russian psychologist Pavel Piskarev and was called neurographic art, although I suppose you will understand that the names are the least of it since we are talking about the same thing. Several studies, such as one conducted by researchers at the University of Wisconsin-Madison, found that participants who took part in neurographic art showed significant improvements in memory and attention, as well as a significant reduction in anxiety and depression symptoms compared to a control group.

Again, you'll paint your emotions, letting the colors and shapes flow freely on the canvas. But then, you'll do something transformative with it. You'll take a soft brush and round off all the sharp corners, softening the lines and hard angles.

This rounding and smoothing process allows energy to flow harmoniously, following the principles of feng shui. The psychology behind rounded corners is based on the way our brain processes visual information.

Rounded corners are associated with feelings of warmth, trust and safety; they do not evoke the same sense of caution or danger as sharp corners. By rounding the corners in your painting, you create a more welcoming and comforting visual space. By softening the edges, you send a message to your subconscious that this is a safe place to explore and process your emotions.

Design and architecture often use rounded corners to create a more welcoming and accessible environment. They are used in childproofing to make sharp corners safe and even in nature, where everything is round and organic.

By rounding the corners in your drawing, you will notice decreased stress and an increased sense of relief from your subconscious. Allow your mind to sink into a state of calm and serenity as your strokes flow smoothly on the paper.

Art Therapy Tool

Perform these exercises when you feel anxiety creeping into your day, and you have the opportunity to sit down and paint.

In addition to these exercises, feel free to paint, draw or engage in any artistic activity in whatever way you wish and in whatever way makes you happy. You will notice how artistic activity can bring you peace and clarity. Develop your artistic expression!

CHAPTER 17
Mindfulness, Meditation

"You should not be led by the dictates of the mind, but the mind should be led by your dictates."

Bhaktivedanta Swami

WHEN WE SPEAK OF meditation, the image of a Buddhist monk in the lotus position, with his eyes closed and an expression of deep peace and serenity on his face, immediately comes to mind. And it is thanks to these devoted practitioners that scientists have been able to study and prove the remarkable changes and benefits that meditation produces in the human brain. They have discovered how this ancient practice can literally reshape your mind for the better.

To do this, they have used modern neuroimaging techniques such as functional magnetic resonance imaging and magnetoencephalography (MEG). These tools allow you to see in detail the activity of different areas of the brain as you meditate. It is possible to observe how certain areas light up and become active while others remain off.

The surprising results obtained during a study at the University of Wisconsin (USA) with Nepalese monk and cell biologist Matthieu Ricard led to him being dubbed "the happiest man on Earth" by the media in 2007. With practice and dedication, it is possible to achieve results similar to those of Matthieu Ricard, taking advantage of the power of your mind to transform your reality.

In the article published by *Scientific American* magazine, Ricard states that through meditation, you have the power to change your mind.

And it's true. You can transform negative thought patterns into positive ones, develop greater awareness of your emotions and reactions, and cultivate qualities such as compassion, equanimity and joy.

The study was conducted over nearly 15 years at the University of Wisconsin, in collaboration with 19 other universities and more than 100 Buddhist monasteries. Images of the brain activity of people with thousands of hours of meditative practice were compared, yielding some fascinating conclusions that will help you understand the benefits of meditation. Through this extensive analysis, it was determined that meditating on a regular basis has the following positive effects on your mind and general well-being:

Anxiety and depression levels decrease noticeably. You will feel a greater sense of calm and emotional balance in your day-to-day life.

Meditating has been shown to reduce the volume of the amygdala, the region of your brain associated with fear processing. By decreasing the activity in this area, you will be able to better manage situations that generate stress and anxiety, responding with greater serenity and mental clarity to them.

Richard Davidson, from the same university, also observed that people with a tendency to depression had greater activation of the right prefrontal area of the brain, while people who better regulated their emotions had more activity in the left.

What's fascinating is that Davidson found that after several weeks of consistent meditation practice, you begin to activate more of that left area associated with emotional well-being. So, every time you meditate, you are training your brain to become more skilled at managing your moods and cultivating positive emotions.

In addition, meditation activates some areas of your brain associated with feelings of empathy and selfless love, allowing you to better connect with others and develop more fulfilling relationships.

Similarly, other studies have revealed that if you meditate regularly over a long period of time, you will have a higher neuronal density, and your brain will stay younger for more years compared to people who do not meditate. It was also observed that meditators' brains had greater roughness, an aspect related to the ability to process information more efficiently. This means that the more you meditate, the more you enhance your mental agility and your ability to analyze and understand the world around you.

Human studies show conclusively that meditation improves executive function and memory. This cognitive sharpening is primarily due to an increase in *brain-derived neurotrophic factor* (BDNF), a key molecule in brain plasticity, learning and memory.

Experienced meditators who participated in a three-month yoga and meditation retreat had three-fold increases in their plasma BDNF levels compared to their pre-retreat levels. And finally, if that's not enough, meditation positively affects telomerase, the enzyme responsible for renewing telomeres, the strands of DNA at the ends of your chromosomes. Every time you meditate, you activate this important enzyme that keeps your cells young and healthy longer. It's like giving your body a natural youth elixir. The more you practice meditation, the more you protect your telomeres and slow down the cellular aging process.

In short, meditation's incredible benefits stem from its ability to reduce stress levels. Every time you meditate, you allow your body and mind to relax deeply, freeing you from pent-up tension. This simple practice triggers a cascade of positive effects on your overall well-being. By decreasing stress, you strengthen your immune system, improve your mental clarity, rejuvenate your cells and much more.

- Helps relax the mind.

- Reduces blood pressure.

- Improves memory.

- Improves emotional stability.

- Improves sleep quality.

- Improves overall health.

- Decreases muscle tension.

- Increases the ability to concentrate.

- Improves mood.

Required Equipment

If meditation were a sport, we would be talking about one of the cheapest and most accessible. It does not require expensive equipment or memberships in exclusive gyms. You can meditate in any quiet place where you can sit or lie down and relax. Whether in a corner of your home, in a peaceful park or even in your office during a break, you have the freedom to create your own meditation space.

The material you need for your practice is minimal: a comfortable chair, a soft cushion or a cozy mat. This simplicity is one of meditation's great advantages, as it allows you to easily incorporate it into your daily routine without much investment or hassle.

If you prefer to adopt an Eastern meditation position, crossing your legs on the floor, you can consider acquiring some accessories specially designed to give you more comfort in your sessions:

The zafu is a special cushion with a round or crescent shape. It is approximately 20 cm high and has a diameter of about 35 cm. It is designed for sitting on, slightly elevating your hips and allowing an upright and stable posture.

You can opt for a zabuton to complement your zafu and add an extra layer of comfort. This is a larger rectangular cushion, approximately 76 x 71 cm, which is placed underneath the zafu. Its function is to provide a cushioned surface for your knees and ankles, preventing them from coming into direct contact with the hard floor, which is especially beneficial if you will be meditating for extended periods of time.

These traditional accessories, while not essential, can make a significant difference in terms of comfort.

It may also be necessary if the room is not at the right temperature to cover yourself with a blanket as your body cools down when meditating. This will help you maintain an optimal body temperature and prevent you from feeling cold, which could distract you from your practice.

If the place is noisy, you may need earplugs to prevent the noise from pulling you out of your state of introspection.

A timer or stopwatch with an alarm will also be a great help to keep track of time without worrying about it, at least in your first few practices.

There are free meditation alarm clocks (meditation timers) for Android and iPhone. I recommend that you download them and program them with the time of each session's exercises. This way, you can customize the duration of your meditations according to your needs and preferences.

How You Should Stand

An incorrect posture can become a constant distraction, preventing you from fully immersing yourself in your meditation practice. Therefore, it is essential that you find a position in which you can remain stable and relaxed throughout the duration of your meditation.

Your body posture conditions your breathing state and, therefore, your mental state. A balanced position will allow you to breathe properly, and your mind will calm down naturally. Find a posture in which you feel comfortable but not too relaxed. Keep your back straight, your shoulders relaxed, and your head upright. Make sure your spine is aligned and that there is no tension in any part of your body.

It is important that you stay in meditation for long periods of time. It's not about staying suffering in acrobatic positions - you're not looking for the perfect photo for Instagram! Forget the images you've seen in magazines and movies of contorted yogis in impossible poses. Your goal is to find a position that allows you to stay focused on your practice.

At the same time, the body should not be overly comfortable, as you may fall asleep. Remember, alertness is one of the essential ingredients of all meditation. It is not about entering a state of drowsiness but about cultivating mindfulness and alertness.

To that end, if you are a Westerner, I suggest two options: the first is to sit in a chair with your back straight and your hands resting on your thighs or folded in your lap. Avoid sinking or slumping into the seat.

The second option is to lie on a mat. Make sure your body is aligned, with your spine straight. You can use a small pillow under your head if needed for comfort. It's not about falling asleep when you meditate, so if you tend to fall asleep easily, the sitting position will be better than lying down.

But ultimately, either option is valid. It is up to you to make the choice based on your own experience and preferences.

In short, the position should allow you to have an upright back and be immobile and comfortable without falling asleep. You must strike a balance between firmness and comfort.

The eyes will be closed, although there are ways to meditate with your eyes open. You can experiment with both options and see which works best for you. Closing your eyes will help you focus inward by reducing external visual distractions. However, if you fall asleep easily, keeping your eyes slightly open, with your gaze relaxed and downward, may be a good alternative.

Once the posture is adopted, the goal is to remain still. Although at first, you will tend to move because you will feel uncomfortable or want to stretch some parts of your body, you should strive to remain still. It is normal to feel discomfort or itching but try not to react to it. To achieve this, you must learn to relax deeply, releasing any unnecessary muscle tension. With practice, you will be able to maintain immobility for longer and longer periods.

Be in Complete Control of Your Attention

The practice of meditation is based on reaching a state of consciousness in which you become an impartial observer of everything that happens in your inner and outer world: bodily sensations, thoughts and emotions. You place yourself in a position of witness without judging or reacting to what you perceive. You simply observe with equanimity and acceptance everything that arises and disappears in the field of your consciousness.

This allows you to distance yourself from the contents of your mind and to see more clearly the transitory nature of all phenomena.

To achieve this, you need to be master of your attention so that you do not allow yourself to be carried away by thoughts that wander into the past or into the future. In a word, you must remain in the here and now: in the present.

And to get your mind in the present moment, the key is breathing. Focus your attention on the simple act of breathing without trying to control or alter it in any way. Fully feel the sensation of the air entering your nose, filling your lungs, and then gently exiting. Focus only on the natural rhythm of your breathing, following each inhalation and exhalation.

It is normal for all kinds of thoughts to arise as you do this. Don't try to block them out or forcibly suppress them. Instead, simply observe them with detachment, as if they were passing clouds in the sky, and let them run their course without getting caught up in them. Don't let those thoughts drag you down or steal your attention from the present moment. Whenever you notice that your mind has become distracted, gently and non-judgmentally bring your attention back to the breath. With practice and patience, you will develop the ability to quiet your mind and stay grounded in the here and now.

Put this way, it sounds easy, but putting it into practice has drawbacks. At first, your mind will resist and want to keep wandering uncontrollably. You will be tempted to give up, thinking that it is impossible to quiet your thoughts. But don't give up. With perseverance and dedication, you will gradually develop the ability to observe your mind without letting it drag you down. Each time you meditate, you will be training your mind to calm down and focus. It will be a gradual process, with advances and setbacks, but if you persevere, the results will surprise you. I must tell you that through practice, you get to tame that wild and unbridled horse that is the mind. That is what meditation is: the art of taming your mind so that it becomes your ally instead of your enemy. So don't be discouraged if it seems difficult at first.

When you cultivate the ability to be present and aware through regular practice, that mental clarity and inner tranquility will be available to you whenever you need it. Whether you are in the midst of the hustle and bustle of the office, enjoying a vacation, connecting with others in deep conversation, or experiencing intimacy with your partner, you will be able to call upon that space of serenity and lucidity within.

The true practice of meditation begins when your mind has achieved this kind of skill. You have learned to quiet your thoughts and focus your attention on the present moment. Such a mind is fully present in the here and now and has the ability to willingly direct its attention to people, thoughts and emotions as needed. This is the true mastery of mindfulness.

Exercise 1: Relaxation Technique

Find a comfortable position, either sitting or lying down, and gently close your eyes. Imagine that you are in a quiet place where you feel safe and comfortable.

Begin by focusing your attention on your breathing. Inhale deeply through your nose, feeling the air fill your lungs and expand your abdomen. Exhale slowly through your mouth, allowing all the air to come out completely. Repeat this process several times, paying attention only to your breathing. Feel how, with each inhalation, vitalizing energy enters and how, with each exhalation, you release tension and sink deeper into a state of calm.

Now, bring your attention to your hands. Feel the tension in your fingers and palms and allow it to dissipate. Imagine your hands becoming heavy and relaxing. Then, allow this feeling of relaxation to travel up your arms, up your wrists, forearms, elbows and finally to your shoulders. Feel each part of your arms relax completely.

Next, turn your attention to your feet. Feel the tension built up in your toes and the soles of your feet. Allow it to dissolve, feeling a pleasant heaviness in your feet. Then, let this feeling of relaxation travel up your legs, up your ankles, calves, knees and thighs. Feel your legs relax and rest completely.

Bring your attention to your back. Imagine each vertebra in your spine relaxing one by one, from your lower back to your neck. Feel your back settle and release any tension. Imagine a warm, soothing sensation running down your spine, giving you a deep sense of relief.

Now, focus on your abdomen. Feel how each inhalation and exhalation relaxes your internal organs. Imagine your abdomen gently expanding and contracting with each breath, releasing any tension. Let this feeling of relaxation spread to your internal organs in the abdominal cavity.

Now, move up into your chest. Feel it relax with each deep breath. Feel your heart beating rhythmically and powerfully. Feel your lungs relaxing and performing their function.

Let the relaxation spread to your neck, releasing any accumulated stiffness. Next, bring your attention to your head. Feel your scalp relax, allowing any tension to dissipate.

Finally, relax your forehead and feel a cool breeze soothing you. Let your eyebrows fall naturally, and let your eyelids feel heavy and relaxed. Your cheeks and lips. Loosen your jaw, leaving a small space between your teeth and dissipating the tension completely.

Remain in this relaxed state for a few moments, enjoying peace and tranquility. If any intrusive thoughts appear, acknowledge them without judgment and let them go, returning your attention to the feeling of relaxation in your body and your breathing.

Enjoy some time in this pleasant state. When you feel ready to finish, begin slowly wriggling your fingers and toes. Gently open your eyes and stretch a little. Then, take the time to return to your daily activities, taking with you the calm and peace you have cultivated in this exercise.

Dedicate a few minutes a day to this practice, and you will notice a significant change in your overall well-being.

Meditation 1: Technique for Being in the Present

Sit in a chair with your back straight or lie down on a mat. Close your eyes and relax your body, allowing all tensions to dissipate. Take a slow, deep breath, allowing the air to fill your lungs. As you exhale, imagine any thoughts or worries fading away as the air leaves your body.

Continue to breathe consciously, focusing on the natural flow of your breath. If any thoughts pop into your mind, observe them without judgment and let them go, returning your attention to the breath.

Take several deep breaths, filling your lungs well and emptying the air well without forcing. Feel how the oxygen floods your body, revitalizing it with each breath. Visualize how, as you breathe in, you are filled with vital energy, a bright and pure light that runs through every cell of your being. As you breathe out, imagine letting go of all your problems, worries, and negativity, letting them go with each exhalation. Gradually, you will notice how your mind calms down and your body relaxes deeply.

Focus on the rhythm of your heart. Use that steady rhythm as a guide for your breathing. For example, you can count six beats as you inhale slowly and deeply, filling your lungs with fresh, revitalizing air. Then, counting another six beats, gently exhale, letting the air out and releasing any tension or stress you may be holding. Adjust the number of beats as you are most comfortable, making sure to keep the same count on both the inhalation and exhalation. The important thing is to find a rhythm that flows naturally and relaxed for you, allowing you to enter a state of calm and serenity.

Then, let the breath become natural and focus your attention on it. You just observe it in an unbiased way. You do nothing but observe.

Observe how the air comes in, how the diaphragm rises, how the air goes out, and how the lungs empty.

Don't think about anything, don't reflect on anything, don't remember images from the past. Just observe, with your attention on the breath.

In this way, you are in the present, in your breathing. However, your mind will try to take you to other places to make you think about things. Each time this happens, and you realize that your attention has been captivated by a thought, begin again the process of watching your breath very closely.

Keep in mind that YOU ARE NOT YOUR MIND OR YOUR THOUGHTS. If you stop identifying with them, sooner or later, your true self will emerge. But this is something you will have to learn and experience for yourself with practice. As you immerse yourself in this process of self-discovery, you will gradually understand the true nature of your being. With patience and dedication, you can detach from the mental patterns that limit you and embrace your authentic essence.

Meditation 2: Non-Attachment Technique

In this exercise, you will allow yourself to go a little further. You are supposed to have mastered perfectly your ability to be in the present and prevent your thoughts from taking you out of it. You have practiced the art of mindfulness, and now you are ready for the next step.

Now, you are going to let your thoughts run wild as if you were watching a movie on the screen of your mind. But remember, you are simply a spectator, watching the flow of ideas without getting attached to them. Keep a healthy distance, knowing at all times that you are not those thoughts but the conscious witness behind them. Do not identify with the mental content; simply observe with curiosity and detachment.

Perceive what is arising in your mind (thoughts, feelings, sounds or emotions) without judgment. Just observe impartially. Notice how each thought appears and fades away, like passing clouds in the sky of your consciousness.

Remain calm without reacting or clinging to any particular idea. Allow your mind to express itself freely, unrestricted and unfiltered. Witness this natural flow with an attitude of acceptance and openness. Remember, you are the serene observer behind all these transitory mental phenomena.

Allow any sensation without judgment, resistance or effort. The essentials of meditation are being aware of what is happening, being lucid, and having complete awareness.

CHAPTER 18

Sexfulness, The Power of Sexuality

"Sex is one of the nine reasons for reincarnation... The other eight are not important."

Henry Miller

CLARA WAS THE MOST organized and efficient person in her circle. At 35, she had succeeded as a marketing manager in a well-known company and had a loyal group of friends, great parents and two siblings with whom she got along very well. However, she felt a constant emptiness inside her.

For months, Clara had been dealing with a growing anxiety. At first, they were small worries that came up from time to time: an important presentation at work, a minor argument with a colleague, or even morning traffic. But over time, these worries grew and multiplied until they became a constant presence in her mind.

Clara's nights were especially difficult. She would lie in her bed, staring at the ceiling, her mind racing a mile a minute. She would often stay up until the wee hours of the morning, mentally reviewing to-do lists, worrying about hypothetical situations, and second-guessing every decision she had made during the day. Her body, in a constant state of alert, reflected her restless mind: headaches, shoulder tension, and a persistent knot in her stomach.

In a casual conversation with her friend Wendy, Clara mentioned what was happening to her. Ever observant and concerned about Clara's well-being, Wendy cut to the chase and asked her about her personal life, especially her relationships and sex life. Clara was surprised by the question but realized that she hadn't had an intimate relationship in over two years. She had been so focused on her work and maintaining a balanced social and family life that she had neglected that part of her life.

Wendy suggested to Clara that she consider the possibility that her lack of a sex life might be contributing to her anxiety. She explained how intimacy and emotional connection, through sex, release tension, improve mood and provide a sense of security. Clara, initially skeptical, decided to do more research on the topic.

In the weeks that followed, Clara read articles and studies on the relationship between sexuality and mental health. She found testimonials from people who, like her, had experienced a significant decrease in their anxiety by rekindling their sex life.

With this new perspective, Clara decided to take steps to improve her situation. She started going out more and meeting new people. Although it was not an instant process, she slowly began to notice changes. Her sleepless nights became less frequent, and her mind felt calmer. The emotional connection she found in her new relationships provided her with the calmness and security she had been missing.

***

Clara's story is a testament to how sexuality influences your mind and your anxiety levels. In the chapter that follows, we will explore in depth how sexuality is one of the most effective tools for reducing anxiety and improving our quality of life.

There is no doubt that your sexuality influences your personal well-being and, specifically, your anxiety levels.

For years, science has explored the profound effects that sexuality has on overall well-being. Through numerous studies, an undeniable connection has been discovered between leading a healthy sex life and enjoying a calmer, happier mind.

In the study *"The Relative Health Benefits of Different Sexual Activities"* by Stuart Brody (2006), it is highlighted that leading a sexually active life is linked to lower levels of stress and anxiety.

Many other studies, such as John Bancroft's *"The Endocrinology of Sexual Arousal"* (2005) or Costa and Brody's *"Sexual Satisfaction, Relationship Satisfaction, and Health"* (2007), reinforce this idea by showing that sexually satisfied people tend to have fewer anxiety and depression problems and enjoy better mental health in general. Feeling connected to your partner through physical intimacy translates into greater happiness and fulfillment in your life.

It's clear that sexuality plays a crucial role in your mental and physical health. It is not just a physical act but a holistic experience that profoundly affects your overall well-being. Recognizing and nurturing your sexuality is a vital step in reducing your anxiety.

But why does this happen? The answer lies in the hormones that are released in your body. During and after sex, your body releases **oxytocin**, known as the "love hormone," and, of course, dopamine.

An embrace, a kiss, a caress or an orgasm produces oxytocin. Every time you share an intimate and affectionate moment with your partner, your body releases this powerful hormone. A simple loving touch can trigger its release, flooding you with a sense of connection. And during sexual climax, oxytocin reaches peak levels, creating a deep bond with your lover.

Oxytocin is exactly what doctors inject intravenously if you're a woman, during labor, when you've been under stress for many hours, and your body isn't producing it naturally. At the climax of labor, oxytocin plays a vitally important role. The hormone will cause the cervix to relax and open, allowing the baby to be born. Without enough oxytocin, labor can become long, painful and complicated.

If you are a woman going into labor, you are in a situation of fear and stress, so you don't naturally produce oxytocin. Your body is tense. That's why the nurse comes in with an injection of synthetic oxytocin to help you through this crucial time. That extra oxytocin will help relax your cervix and allow it to open up, making it easier for your baby to be born. It's a little push your body needs to overcome the blockage of fear and stress and embrace the miracle of life to come.

It is sometimes called the "love hormone," as it has been found to be a bonding hormone in humans and other mammals and to play a key role in sensuality, affection and sexuality. However, oxytocin is important in romantic love and the bond between parents and children. Babies who are abandoned in an orphanage and do not receive the physical contact necessary to stimulate the production of oxytocin may decide to stop eating because they do not want to live without this substance that gives them the feeling of security and love.

The important thing is that you realize that having a full affective and sexual life is something very desirable because you produce oxytocin, and this will help you to significantly reduce your anxiety and stress levels.

And now I want to introduce you to a concept that may be new to you: *sexfulness*.

The key to sexuality lies in your attitude, in the state of mind with which you approach sex and love.

Cultivating the right attitude in any facet of life is essential, so why should it be any different in your love life? Your approach and perspective are key in determining the quality of your sexual and romantic experiences. Adopting a positive, open and conscious mindset will completely transform the way you experience and enjoy love and intimacy.

It is easier to understand the meaning of *sexfulness* if you understand where the idea came from, although you may have already glimpsed it because of its similarity to another popular concept. The term *mindfulness* was popularized in the West by Jon Kabat-Zinn, a professor emeritus of medicine who integrated some of his Zen, yoga and Buddhism practices with concepts from Western science, creating the REBAP (Mindfulness-Based Stress Reduction) technique and the Stress Reduction Clinic. This practice involves being fully present and aware in the moment, without judgment, something you can apply not only to meditation but to all areas of your life, including your sexuality.

I define the concept of *sexfulness* as "full sexuality," or what is the same as a "state of full sexual attention," whose foundation consists of reaching a high level of attention to your bodily sensations, thoughts and emotions, without judging whether they are correct or not, at the moment of your sexual experience. It is about being fully present in your sexual experience, living in the here and now with an open and receptive mind.

The goal of full sexuality is to connect with your inner essence and to react more consciously and effectively to the sexual events in your life. By practicing conscious sexuality, you can learn to enjoy your sexuality more fully, overcome blocks or inhibitions, and deepen your connection with your partner. It is a path to a more satisfying and fulfilling sex life.

Call to Action: Energize Your Sex Life

It's time to step up and start integrating this practice into your daily life as part of your anti-anxiety therapy. If you have a partner, it's critical that you talk to them. Open and honest communication is key. Sit down with your partner and honestly discuss your feelings and desires. Share your concerns and everything you've learned about the benefits of sexual practice for anxiety. Explain how you think a more active and mindful sex life could help you better manage your anxiety and improve your overall well-being. Listen to his or her thoughts and concerns about this as well.

Establishing a dedicated time for intimacy is crucial to your relationship and your own well-being. Just as you set aside time for other forms of self-care, such as exercising, meditating or reading a good book, you should also make sure there is regular time to connect with your partner without distractions. Look for times when you can both relax and enjoy each other's company, whether it's a date night, a sensual massage, or just cuddling and talking. This time, doesn't have to follow a rigid plan, but it should be a priority in your schedule.

The environment plays an important role in this experience. Make sure it is relaxing and inviting. Candles, soft music or even a little aromatherapy, can transform any place into a love nest. Choose colors and textures that make you feel at peace and at ease. Perhaps some fluffy cushions, soft linens and dim lighting. Create an atmosphere that invites intimacy and enjoyment of the senses—a space where you can leave the stress of the day behind and fully immerse yourself in the present moment with your partner.

Don't be afraid to explore and experiment. Intimacy doesn't have just one way of expressing itself. You can explore different ways to connect with your partner, whether it's through sensual massage, role-playing that sparks your imagination, or any other activity that makes you both feel comfortable. Allow yourselves to be creative and spontaneous. Let your curiosity guide you to discover new ways to enjoy each other.

Always remember that consent and mutual respect are fundamental. Sexual practice should always be consensual and respectful.

If you do not have a partner, this can be an excellent time to open yourself to new opportunities. The search for a partner can be an adventure in itself, allowing you to meet someone special with whom to share these intimate moments. Consider joining social activities where you can interact with like-minded people, sign up for dating sites that fit your values, or simply be open to meeting new people in your day-to-day life. Keep your eyes and heart open, be authentic in your interactions and allow things to flow naturally. Don't force anything; enjoy the process of meeting others. The key is to maintain a positive, receptive and patient attitude. Trust that you will find that special person when the time is right.

Also, while looking for a partner, self-exploration is a valuable tool for reducing anxiety. Spend time getting to know yourself better, discovering your tastes, passions, and what makes you tick. Masturbation not only releases endorphins that improve your mood, but it will also help you better understand your body and your desires. This self-knowledge will not only help you reduce anxiety but will also prepare you for a future relationship, as you will be able to better communicate your needs and desires to your partner.

If you want to go deeper into these concepts, I invite you to look for some of my books that go in-depth into sexual practice from a tantric perspective. In them, you will find concrete techniques and exercises to incorporate conscious sexuality into your life easily and effectively. You will learn to connect with your body, to listen to your deepest desires and to experience pleasure from a place of presence and acceptance.

The important thing now is for you to recognize that sex is a key factor in reducing your anxiety levels. Don't see it as something secondary or dispensable but as a powerful tool to balance your mind and emotions.

Start incorporating conscious sexuality into your life today and discover the power it has to transform your mental well-being, reducing your anxiety levels naturally and effectively!

CHAPTER 19

Bibliotherapy or Reading Books

"Reading a good book is a constant dialogue in which the book speaks and the soul responds."

Anonymous

CARLOS WORKED AT A technology company in New York, where he faced tight deadlines, multiple projects and fierce competition. Stress began to affect his work performance, his personal life and his health, and he was on the verge of burnout.

That's when he heard about bibliotherapy, a technique a colleague had used to manage his own stress. Intrigued and desperate to find a solution, Carlos decided to give it a try.

His journey began with "The Shadow of the Wind" by Carlos Ruiz Zafón. From the first chapter, he was caught up in the mystery and beauty of the narrative. Every night, after a tiring day at work, he would read a few pages until he fell asleep. The magical atmosphere of Barcelona and the intriguing plot transported him away from his daily worries.

As Carlos became more involved in the story, he noticed that his anxiety diminished. Daniel Sempere's adventures offered him an escape, a mental respite. Motivated by the positive impact of the first book, he decided to go further.

His next choice was "The Catcher in the Rye" by J.D. Salinger. This book offered him a different view of life through the eyes of young Holden Caulfield. The protagonist's sometimes chaotic narration resonated with Charles, helping him understand and process his own feelings of stress and confusion.

Over time, reading became a daily habit for Charles. Not only did he read to escape, but he also found the characters and their stories a source of reflection and wisdom.

"To Kill a Mockingbird" by Harper Lee was another book that had a profound impact on him. Atticus Finch's bravery and Scout's innocence reminded him of the importance of empathy and justice, values that he began to integrate more into his daily life.

Through reading, Carlos began to develop new points of view and greater empathy for others, which also improved his relationships. The stories and characters offered him refuge and valuable lessons that he applied in his day-to-day life.

After several months of bibliotherapy, Carlos noticed significant changes in his life. His stress level had decreased considerably. He felt calmer, more focused and better able to cope with the pressures of his job. In addition, his health improved: he slept better and had more energy.

A year later, Carlos reflected on his journey and realized how his life had changed because he had adopted the habit of reading. Bibliotherapy not only helped him manage his stress but also provided him with tools to improve his overall emotional and mental well-being. Inspired by his own transformation, he began sharing his experience with friends and colleagues, recommending novels that had helped him.

Carlos improved his life thanks to bibliotherapy, demonstrating that sometimes the answer to our greatest challenges can be found in small changes.

***

Don't think that Carlos is the only one who has found a way out of his problems through reading. Remember the last time you were completely immersed in the pages of a captivating book? Suddenly, the world around you faded away, leaving only you and the story that enveloped you. That is the extraordinary power of reading, a power that transcends mere entertainment.

Amid the daily hustle and bustle, where stress and pressure seem constant, reading provides an oasis of calm and reflection—an intimate space where you can take refuge and find yourself again.

I invite you to reflect on an exciting subject from both the scientific and the human angle: the influence that the habit of reading has on your psychological well-being.

Numerous studies have confirmed what you already sensed: reading is not only a pleasure, but also brings extraordinary benefits to your mind.

A 2009 study by neuroscientists and psychologists at the University of Sussex revealed that regular reading reduced stress levels by a staggering 68%. This figure even surpassed other popular relaxation techniques, such as listening to soothing music or enjoying a comforting cup of tea in a pleasant environment.

Dr. David Lewis, the neuropsychologist who conducted the study, said, *"It really doesn't matter what book you read. By losing yourself in an absorbing book, you can escape the worries and stresses of the everyday world and spend some time exploring the world of the author's imagination."*

When you are reading a gripping novel, the characters come alive, and their experiences become your own as you get deeper into the plot. Suddenly, your own tensions and anxieties seem to fade away, temporarily relegated to the background. Your mind is freed from the burden of unsettling thoughts and completely gives itself to the story.

This state of immersion not only provides a respite from stress but also revitalizes your brain. Immersing yourself in a different world allows your mind to rest and recuperate. It's like giving your brain a mini-vacation from the relentless demands of daily life.

After this mental break, you will notice that your cognitive abilities are revitalized. Your concentration improves, your creativity sharpens, and your ability to face everyday challenges grows.

***

Reading not only provides a break from stress but also actively strengthens your brain. Every time you immerse yourself in a book, you create new neural connections. These connections are essential for maintaining medium and long-term brain health, and act as a protective shield against age-related degenerative diseases such as Alzheimer's and dementia.

However, the impact of reading goes beyond the cognitive; it also profoundly affects one's emotional life. When one reads, one not only passively processes information but also becomes immersed in the characters' experiences. One becomes their traveling companion, sharing their joys, struggles, triumphs and defeats.

A 2011 study conducted at the University at Buffalo by psychologists Shira Gabriel and Ariana Young revealed that those who read regularly are more able to understand and relate to others. Reading fiction, in particular, allows you to put yourself in other people's shoes and experience a wide range of emotions and social situations. This process of "living other lives" through the pages of a book strengthens your empathy, an essential quality for building and maintaining healthy relationships.

Bibliotherapy, or the therapeutic use of reading, is an increasingly recognized approach in psychotherapy. Through carefully selected books, patients can find a mirror for their own experiences, see examples of how others face similar challenges, and discover effective strategies for navigating difficult situations.

This therapeutic modality will be particularly beneficial if you feel alone in your personal battles. You will find comfort in realizing that you are not alone and others have experienced similar situations.

Call to Action: Book Therapy

Discover the power of reading to calm the mind and reduce anxiety! By making reading a daily habit, you will experience a remarkable transformation. Your mind will expand, your perspective will broaden, and your ability to face life's challenges will strengthen.

So, I encourage you to incorporate this habit into your daily routine, even if it's just dedicating a few minutes each day to reading!

CHAPTER 20
Creative Visualization

"Vision without action is a daydream. Action without vision is a nightmare."

Japanese proverb

THE SUN WAS BEGINNING to set behind the mountains, tinting the sky with orange and pink tones. Carla sat on her balcony, watching the horizon with a cup of tea. It had been a long day, full of meetings and endless responsibilities that had kept her on the verge of collapse. She took a deep breath, trying to relax her tense muscles. Nervous tension had been her inseparable companion for the past few years, ever-present, always lurking.

She remembered her therapist's advice, "Try to visualize yourself as a calm, anxiety-free person." At first, the idea struck her as strange and unrealistic. How could she imagine something so distant from her current reality and expect it to bring her peace of mind? However, after a few sleepless nights and tense days, she decided to give it a try.

She closed her eyes and began to breathe deeply. She imagined she was in her favorite place: a clearing in the middle of the forest with a small lake. But this time, instead of just visualizing the surroundings, she visualized herself walking along the path that led to the clearing. She observed every detail: her upright posture, serene face, and slow, confident movements.

She saw herself smiling, breathing calmly, and enjoying the moment without rushing.

As she progressed in her visualization, Carla noticed how the tension in her shoulders and neck began to disappear. She saw herself sitting by the lake, contemplating her reflection in the crystal-clear water. In her reflection, she did not see the tense, worried woman she used to be but a calm, confident version of herself, at peace with herself. The Carla, in the reflection, was not overwhelmed by her thoughts but was enjoying the here and now.

Every time her mind tried to wander to the day's worries, she would refocus on that image of herself, reminding herself that this calm and serene person was also her. With each visualization, that image became clearer and more real.

The sun had already set when she opened her eyes, and the first stars began shining in the sky. Surprised, she realized that her heart was beating more calmly and her mind was clear. She felt in control of the situation for the first time in a long time.

Throughout the days and weeks that followed, Carla continued to practice visualization. It became her refuge, a place she could turn to whenever anxiety threatened to visit. Not only did she find comfort in those moments of visualization, but she also began to notice changes in her daily life. Situations that had previously paralyzed her were now more manageable, and her confidence grew with each visualization session.

Visualization had become a powerful tool for Carla, a way to cope with her anxiety and reclaim her life. This technique, which had initially seemed simple and ineffective, proved to be one of the keys to her well-being and inner peace.

Carla smiled, knowing that she had found a way to overcome her anxiety, step by step, visualization after visualization.

***

Imagine for a moment that you are about to give an important speech. You stand in front of the podium, looking out at the expectant crowd. Just by visualizing the scene, your heart begins to beat faster, your palms sweat, and you feel a knot in your stomach. Anxiety takes over, making your hands tremble slightly as you hold your notes. You take deep breaths, trying to calm your nerves, but the feeling of panic persists. This is living proof that your thoughts have the power to trigger intense physical responses, even when the threat is not real and the speech has not yet begun. The good news is that, just as you can use visualization to generate anxiety, you can also use it to create a state of calm and confidence.

Neuroimaging studies have shown that the areas of the brain that are activated during the visualization of a scene are the same ones that are activated during the actual experience. For example, suppose you visualize that you are running. In that case, the motor regions of your brain that are activated are the same ones that would be activated if you were actually running. This means that your mind has the power to simulate experiences so vividly that your body responds as if they were actually happening.

It's as if our brains can't distinguish between what's real and what's imagined. This phenomenon is called brain activation, which is why visualization is so effective.

Psychic visualization consists of imagining situations you want to experience and projecting them into the future to better live in the present. It is about thinking in images in a clear and sharp way, seeing yourself, and experiencing those desired situations and sensations.

Suppose you have to face a situation that would cause you anxiety, such as speaking in front of a group of people or meeting new people at a party. Instead of allowing anxiety to take over, close your eyes and immerse yourself in a psychic visualization session.

Visualize a version of yourself in that same situation, but this time, you look calm, confident and in control of the situation. Notice how you interact with others, how your posture is erect, and your voice is steady. Feel your confidence radiating, and watch how you move with grace and ease.

Pay attention to the details: the smile on your face, the sense of comfort that envelops you. Allow these images to become increasingly clear and real in your mind.

As you immerse yourself in this visualization, your brain forms new neural connections. These connections associate the situation that previously caused you anxiety with feelings of calm and security. The more you practice this technique, the stronger this association becomes.

Psychic visualization is a powerful tool for reprogramming your mind and transforming your relationship with anxiety. By projecting positive, uplifting images of yourself facing challenging situations, you are sending a clear message to your subconscious: "I am capable of handling this with calmness and confidence."

Each time you visualize yourself succeeding in situations that normally generate anxiety for you, you will be one step closer to turning that vision into reality. Your mind will begin to look for opportunities to replicate those images in your daily life, mobilizing your inner resources to achieve your goals.

Spend a few minutes each day immersing yourself in these positive images, preferably before going to sleep, and watch how, little by little, your reality begins to reflect the confidence and peace of mind you've cultivated in your thoughts.

Your imagination is a powerful tool. Use it wisely to sculpt the life you desire, free from the constraints of anxiety. With each visualization, you move one step closer to becoming the best version of yourself.

When you practice psychic visualization, you don't just use images. You can use all your senses: imagining sounds, smells and tactile sensations can make the visualization even more effective. This makes the experience more realistic and helps your brain and body respond more efficiently.

In short, psychic visualization is a tool that connects the mind and body, activating the brain in a way similar to real experiences. Regular practice will help you manage anxiety more effectively, promoting greater calm and control in your daily life.

Psychic Visualization Exercise

Now, I will guide you step-by-step through a creative psychic visualization session that will transform your life. Get ready to embark on an inner journey that will awaken your full potential.

First of all, you must be in a state of deep relaxation so that your brain will better assimilate the sensations you experience during the visualization. It is as if you were opening a direct door to your subconscious, allowing positive images and emotions to be recorded with greater intensity.

Find a quiet, comfortable place where you won't be interrupted. Sit or lie down in a position that allows you to relax completely. Breathe deeply, allowing the air to fill your lungs and then slowly let it out. With each exhalation, feel the tension dissipate from your body.

When you feel completely relaxed, gently close your eyes. Now, visualize yourself in a situation you would like to be in or imagine the accomplishment you wish to achieve. Choose a scene that you find particularly pleasing and stimulating.

As you immerse yourself in this visualization, pay attention to all the details. Allow your senses to be fully activated, experiencing every tactile sensation, every scent and every emotion associated with that moment.

Don't rush. Take as much time as you need to build a clear and vivid picture in your mind. When you have the desired scene clear, think of it in the present tense, as if it were happening here and now. Feel the excitement and satisfaction of living that moment, of having achieved that goal.

To further enhance the effect of the visualization, imagine moving scenes instead of static images. Visualize yourself interacting with the environment, moving with confidence and fluidity. Observe how you perform in that situation and how you enjoy every moment.

Dedicate about 10 minutes to this practice, repeating the scene several times to reinforce its impact on your subconscious mind. Remember that repetition is the key to creating new habits and new neural connections.

Let yourself become fully immersed in the experience, letting the positive sensations wash over you.

It is excellent to practice this exercise just before going to sleep. When you are in that state of deep relaxation called alpha, right at the threshold of sleep, your mind is more receptive to suggestions and visualizations. If you fall asleep while doing so, your subconscious will be impacted even more powerfully.

Happy visualizations and happy dreams!

CHAPTER 21

Music Therapy

"I think music in itself is healing. It's an explosive expression of humanity. It's something we are all touched by. No matter what culture we're from, everyone loves music."

Billy Joel

ONE DAY, AFTER A *particularly hard day at work, Sofia collapsed on her couch, feeling her mind was about to explode. She decided to search the Internet for alternative methods to relieve her stress. That's when she came across an article on music therapy. Intrigued, she read about how music could calm the mind and reduce anxiety. She remembered how much she had loved music in her youth before the responsibilities of adult life overwhelmed her.*

Determined to try something new, Sofia signed up for music therapy sessions at a local center. The first session was eye-opening. The therapist, a kind man named David, welcomed her into a softly lit room filled with musical instruments of all kinds. "Music has the power to heal," David told her, "but you must be open to letting it take you."

Sophia began with passive listening to music. David provided her with a carefully selected playlist of soft, soothing melodies. At first, she was skeptical. She lay down on a mat, closed her eyes and let the music flow through her. She felt the tension in her body slowly melt away as if the music was absorbing them.

Eventually, Sofia moved on to creating and composing music. Although she had never played an instrument before, David encouraged her to experiment. She began playing the piano awkwardly at first but soon found expressing herself through the keys liberating. Each note she played seemed to take away a piece of her anxiety, replacing it with a sense of peace.

One of Sofia's most transformative moments came during a musical improvisation session. David handed her a drum and asked her to play whatever she felt. At first, she felt self-conscious but soon lost her fear. She closed her eyes and let her hands move freely. She hit the drum hard, releasing years of pent-up tension. When she finished, tears streamed down her face, but they were tears of relief.

Vocalizing and singing also became part of her therapy. David encouraged her to sing, no matter what, as long as she felt it. Sofia rediscovered the pleasure of singing in the shower and humming while working. Her voice, which she had always considered ordinary, became a powerful tool for releasing her emotions.

Outside of the sessions, Sofia incorporated music therapy into her daily life. She created personalized playlists for each moment: a relaxing playlist for mornings, an energetic one for work and a calming one for the evening. She even used therapeutic music apps to meditate before bedtime.

Gradually, Sofia noticed significant changes in her life. Her constant anxiety began to diminish. She felt calmer, more focused and able to handle stress. Even her work improved; her creativity flowed more freely without being clouded by uncontrolled thinking.

***

This is going to be a very short chapter, as everyone knows the benefits of listening to music. It will just be a reminder that you have a powerful and pleasant tool for combating stress and anxiety.

Music has an almost magical power over emotions. When you listen to music that pleases you, your brain releases serotonin and dopamine, generating feelings of pleasure and reward similar to those you experience when you eat your favorite foods or receive praise. Those melodies and rhythms you enjoy so much can elevate your mood and make you feel more relaxed and happier.

Music activates several areas of your brain, including those related to emotion, memory and movement. For example, your amygdala, crucial for emotional processing, responds strongly when you hear melodies that move you.

Music has the power to evoke vivid memories and awaken deep emotions in you. It can instantly transport you to happy moments in the past or help you process difficult feelings in the present. It can even prompt your body to move to the beat through dancing or simply following the cadence with your foot.

Numerous scientific research studies have backed up these effects, and a proper music session is known to significantly reduce cortisol levels, the stress hormone. When you immerse yourself in your favorite songs, you feel the tension melt away, and a sense of calm comes over you.

A study conducted by the University of Marburg in Germany found that music therapy reduced anxiety levels in patients preparing for surgery. Imagine the power of music to help you face challenging situations with greater serenity.

In addition to stress reduction, music therapy improves mood. Upbeat, energizing music lifts the mood and provides a temporary emotional escape. Soft, melodic songs induce a state of calm and tranquility, perfect for moments of relaxation and meditation.

If you decide to use music to calm your mind, you can do so in various ways, depending on the degree of connection you enjoy with it.

Passive Music Therapy: Listening to Selected Music

Listening to specially selected music induces states of relaxation and reduces your anxiety.

Music selection is essential and should be tailored to your individual tastes and responses. Generally, you should choose soft instrumental music that resonates with you, such as classical pieces, nature sounds or ambient music. Avoid fast rhythms and complex lyrics that may distract or agitate you. Experiment with different genres and artists until you find the perfect combination that helps you calm your mind.

If you prefer to enjoy structured sessions with a therapist, the therapist can guide you through deep breathing exercises while you listen to music specially selected for you.

You can also benefit from guided meditation recordings that combine listening to music with relaxation and meditation exercises to create a state of deep peace in the tranquility of your home. They are extremely effective in reducing anxiety, as they induce a state of deep relaxation and decrease physiological stress.

Another powerful tool in music therapy that you can also use is meditation with binaural sounds. These sounds use the difference in frequency between two slightly different tones, one in each ear, to produce a third frequency that your brain perceives.

When you hear two tones of slightly different frequencies, one in each ear, your brain detects the difference between them and creates a new frequency that is the difference between the two original ones. For example, if a 300 Hz tone is played in one ear and a 310 Hz tone in the other ear, your brain will perceive a binaural beat of 10 Hz.

This perceived frequency synchronizes with your brainwaves through a process called frequency entrainment, inducing states of deep relaxation, concentration, creativity, deep sleep and others.

This fascinating technique can help you induce different beneficial mental states, such as deep relaxation, increased concentration and restful sleep.

Active Music Therapy: Unleash Your Creativity

If you choose active music therapy, you will be directly involved in creating music, whether playing instruments, singing or improvising. This form of therapy invites you to explore your innate creativity. You do not need previous musical experience; simply let yourself be carried away by the sounds and sensations that arise within you.

Playing an instrument such as a guitar, piano, or even a simple drum will help you connect with yourself. Singing can be tremendously cathartic, releasing repressed feelings. You can also write lyrics and compose melodies that reflect your experiences. Musical improvisation fosters spontaneity and confidence.

Whatever your skill level, active music therapy promotes creative self-expression. It invites you to let go of perfectionism and simply enjoy the process. When you make music from the heart, without worrying about the end result, you flow and are present.

Allow yourself to explore different instruments and musical styles. Use accessible and easy-to-play instruments, such as drums, xylophones and maracas. Let yourself be carried away by the melody and rhythm, and watch your mind quiet as you immerse yourself in the experience. It's not about creating a masterpiece but about connecting with your inner self through the sounds. Embrace the freedom to express yourself without judgment or expectation and discover the joy of creating music for pure pleasure.

So don't be afraid. Music therapy, both passive and active, is a powerful tool to connect with yourself, reduce stress and anxiety, and find a new way to communicate your emotions. Let the healing sounds of music guide you to a place of calm, joy and well-being.

Here are some examples of types of music that can be helpful to you on your path to inner healing. From soft, soothing melodies to joyful, energizing beats, there is a wide variety of musical genres that can help you connect with your emotions and find peace in the midst of chaos. However, take these examples only as a guideline and find the music that you really connect with and that resonates with you. Explore different artists, styles and eras until you find those special songs that make you feel good, inspire you and fill you with positivity. Remember that music is a personal journey, and what works for one may not work for another. Trust your intuition and let yourself be guided by the sounds that call to you.

Relaxing Classical Music:

Ludovico Einaudi: His piano compositions, such as "*Nuvole Bianche*" and "*Divenire,*" are calming and emotional.

Claude Debussy: "*Clair de Lune*" and "*Arabesque No. 1*" are perfect examples of soft and relaxing music.

Erik Satie: "*Gymnopédies*" are ideal for inducing a state of relaxation.

Ambient Music

Brian Eno: Albums such as "*Music for Airports*" and "*Ambient 1: Music for Airports*" are perfect for creating a peaceful atmosphere.

Hildegard von Bingen: Medieval music that combines ethereal vocalizations with natural ambient sounds.

Sounds of Nature

At Sound Healing Center, they offer you recordings of natural sounds such as ocean waves, rain and birdsong, which are perfect for deep relaxation.

Music of Mantras and Spiritual Chanting

Snatam Kaur: Her mantras and chants, such as *"Ong Namo"* and *"Mul Mantra,"* are widely used in yoga and meditation sessions.

Krishna Das: Known for his kirtans and bhajans, such as *"Om Namah Shivaya."*

Platforms to Access Guided Meditations in English

Fortunately, today, you can access a wide variety of platforms that offer meditations in English, specifically designed to help you relax and manage anxiety.

YouTube is an excellent source for you to find a wide variety of music, mantra chants, guided meditations and binaural sounds. You can search for specific channels dedicated to meditation or explore playlists created by other users.

Spotify is also a good option for discovering guided meditation playlists in English. Many compilations are available, ranging from short mindfulness sessions to longer meditations for deep relaxation.

There are meditation apps like Calm, Insight Timer, and Headspace that also offer you options in Spanish. These apps allow you to easily access guided meditations on your phone anytime, anywhere.

Music Therapy Tool

Add specific moments to your weekly schedule to enjoy music therapy in any of its modalities!

CHAPTER 22
Spiritual Level

IN THE SPIRITUAL WORLD, you encounter the highest levels of your existence. It is on this plane that you discover the source of your divine connection and your true spiritual essence.

As you step into this level, you experience a deep connection to the eternal and the absolute that transcends all limitations of the physical and emotional world.

Here, you discover that you are a divine spark, an eternal and immortal part that links you deeply with the totality of the universe.

This connection allows you to rise to a higher state of consciousness, where wisdom and intuition flow naturally and spontaneously.

The spiritual world is the home of true wisdom. It is your path to enlightenment, helping you to understand and apply universal truths in your daily life. It is a place of inner peace where you find answers to your deepest questions and discover your higher purpose. By allowing this wisdom to flow through you, you become more conscious and in harmony with the universe.

You realize that you are much more than your physical body and thoughts; you are an extension of the infinite, a unique expression of the divine energy that permeates all existence.

On this plane, limitations fade away, and you open yourself to unlimited possibilities, realizing your true potential and purpose in life.

Accessing this level of existence not only brings you peace and clarity but also propels you to radically transform your life. It motivates you to align with your deepest values and to live with a clear and defined purpose.

CHAPTER 23
Helping Others

"The best way to find yourself is to lose yourself in the service of others."

Mahatma Gandhi

Isabel was trapped in an endless cycle of anguish. Every day seemed like an emotional roller coaster, and she didn't know how to stop it.

One day, while walking to work, Isabel saw an elderly woman struggling to cross the street with several shopping bags. Without a second thought, she ran to help her. The elderly woman gratefully smiled at her and said, "Thank you, my dear. You have made my day so much easier today." That small act of kindness brightened Elizabeth's day more than she could have imagined.

Intrigued by the sense of peace she experienced, Isabel decided to try something new. Instead of focusing on her own problems, she began to look for opportunities to help others. She volunteered at a soup kitchen on weekends, listened carefully to her friends when they needed to talk and began doing small, random acts of kindness, such as paying for the coffee of the person behind her in line.

Over time, Isabel noticed something surprising. Her anxiety began to diminish. By focusing on the needs of others, her mind had less room for the personal worries that used to consume her. She felt more connected to her community and less isolated in her thoughts.

One of the most impactful moments for Isabel occurred in the soup kitchen. She was serving dinner when an older man, clearly going through hard times, tearfully thanked her. "You don't know how much this means to me," he told her. "This is the first hot dish I've had in days." In that instant, she realized the power of empathy. Not only was she helping others, but she was also helping herself.

Elizabeth understood that by turning her attention away from her worries to the well-being of others, she was creating a virtuous circle of kindness and gratitude. Her anxiety did not disappear completely, but it became manageable, and the panic episodes decreased dramatically. She discovered that the real magic of empathy lay in its ability to connect people, alleviate suffering and, surprisingly, calm her own.

Today, Isabel continues to practice empathy in her daily life. She knows that the key to keeping her anxiety under control lies not in fighting it but in expanding her heart and helping others.

***

Anxiety has a cunning way of trapping you in your thoughts, like an invisible web that wraps around you without you even realizing it. It makes you focus all your attention on your problems, creating an endless cycle of worry and distress that seems to have no way out. Have you ever felt trapped in this loop, like you're in a mental maze from which you can't escape?

A 2013 study published in the *Journal of Affective Disorders* found that people with high levels of anxiety tend to focus more on their own problems and less on others. Other research, published in the *Journal of Anx-*

iety, Stress & Coping in 2017, showed that going over and over the same thoughts and self-centeredness not only increases anxiety but decreases your ability to empathize and connect with others.

Maria, 28: *"When my anxiety was at its peak, I was stuck in my thoughts all the time. I couldn't stop thinking about my mistakes and what could go wrong. This made me feel even more anxious and isolated, as I couldn't focus on the needs of the people around me."*

Carlos, 35, experienced something similar: *"The anxiety made me feel like I was in a bubble. I was so obsessed with my fears and worries that I couldn't see what was happening in other people's lives. This only made my anxiety worse, as I felt disconnected and alone."*

This is where the transformative power of empathy comes in. Empathy is the ability to understand and share another person's feelings. It's not just about feeling compassion but about putting yourself in the other person's shoes and seeing the world from their point of view. This change of perspective is liberating.

When you focus on the needs and feelings of others, you put aside your problems. This shift of focus breaks the anxiety loop as you occupy your mind with other issues instead of your worries. You free yourself from the mental prison of your obsessive thoughts.

In addition, practicing empathy strengthens social connections. By putting yourself in the other person's shoes and providing genuine support, you build deeper, more meaningful relationships. In turn, the social support you cultivate becomes a powerful buffer against stress and anxiety.

Let's take examples of acts of empathy that have positively impacted people's anxiety.

Volunteering at a charity, for example, can be a transformative experience. Imagine spending a few hours a week at a soup kitchen or animal shelter.

This connection to a cause greater than yourself benefits those you help and nurtures your emotional well-being.

You may be surprised to discover, as Isabel was, that actively listening to your friends will strengthen your relationships and provide a healthy distraction from your recurring thoughts.

John, who suffered from social anxiety, found relief by participating in support groups. Listening to the experiences of others developed his empathy and significantly decreased his anxiety.

In summary, practicing empathy and focusing on the needs of others is a powerful tool for combating anxiety. Start today. Practice an act of empathy and watch how your world begins to change.

Have you ever wondered how you can contribute to making the world a better place? The answer is simple: be kind to a stranger every day! Yes, that's right, small acts of kindness can have a huge impact—be creative and discover the transformative power of kindness!

Here are some inspiring ideas for practicing kindness, but I'm sure you'll find many more.

Surprise with a Thank You Card: Write a thank you card and leave it on the windshield of a random car. A few kind words can unexpectedly brighten someone's day.

Give Flowers: Buy a bouquet of flowers and hand them out to people you meet on your way, such as the cleaning staff, a co-worker or even a stranger on the street. A flower can brighten anyone's day.

Donate Unworn Clothes: Go through your closet and donate clothes you no longer wear to a charity. A forgotten item of yours can be a great help to someone else.

Help Someone with Their Shopping: If you see someone at the grocery store with a full shopping cart, offer to help them load their groceries into the car. This simple act can make a big difference, especially for seniors or mothers with young children.

Share a Book: Leave a book you really enjoyed in a public place with a note that says, "Read to me and pass it on to someone else when you're done." This act not only shares knowledge but also a rewarding experience.

The magic of these acts of kindness lies in the karmic principle that "what goes around comes around." When you start doing random acts of kindness, more kindness will come back to you! This virtuous cycle not only benefits others but also fills you with a profound sense of well-being. It is true that empathy, like anything else, must be balanced, that is, without forgetting yourself.

If you want to improve the world, start with yourself.

Call to Action: Do Something Small for Others

Commit to doing one random act of kindness every day for the next two weeks. Watch what happens, but don't expect anything in return. Kindness always finds its way back!

Start Today!

CHAPTER 24
The Power of Praying

"If you know how to gain the cooperation of Akashic Intelligence in your life, you will have a life full of blessings."
Sadhguru

Lucia was a single mother dedicated to her young children, Sofia and Mateo. She worked all day as a nurse at a local hospital to ensure a comfortable life for them. However, the weight of her responsibilities and constant worries began to take a deep toll on her.

Lucia had always been a strong woman, but lately, her mind was filled with obsessive thoughts that paralyzed her. She feared for her children's safety every time they left the house, and her anxiety about their well-being kept her awake at night.

She checked the door locks and windows several times before bed and constantly called the school to ensure her children were okay. These thoughts gave her no rest, affecting her sleep and overall well-being.

Desperate to find relief, Lucia decided to go to church, a place she had attended as a child but had stopped attending over the years. She remembered the peace she felt in the church pews and decided it was time to seek spiritual help. It was then that she met Father Ildefonso, her parish priest.

Father Ildefonso welcomed her into his office with a warm smile and eyes full of compassion. Lucia, with tears in her eyes, told him about the obsessive thoughts that were tormenting her and how they were affecting her life.

Father Ildefonso listened to her attentively and then, in a soft, serene voice, said, "Lucia, the mind can be a stormy place, but there is a peace to be found beyond our thoughts. Prayer can be a powerful tool for finding that peace."

Lucia felt skeptical but hopeful. She was willing to try anything to ease her torment. Father Ildefonso taught her a simple yet profound prayer: a prayer of surrender and trust in God. He also suggested that she spend a few minutes each day in contemplative prayer, focusing on God's presence and allowing divine peace to fill her mind and heart.

After putting her children to bed that night, Lucia knelt by her bedside, as Father Ildefonso had taught her. She closed her eyes and began to pray: "Lord, I place my fears and worries in your hands. Please give me the peace that only you can give. Help me to trust in Your love and rest in Your presence."

The first few days were difficult. The obsessive thoughts were still there, but Lucia noticed brief moments of tranquility. *She persisted with prayer, remembering the priest's words about the importance of constancy and surrender.*

One Sunday after Mass, Lucia approached Father Ildefonso and shared her progress. *"Father, I still have obsessive thoughts, but I notice that they are not as intense as before. Sometimes, during prayer, I feel a peace that I have never experienced before."*

The priest smiled and encouraged her to keep going. He reminded her that prayer is a process, a path to a deeper relationship with God and with herself. He suggested that she supplement her prayer with reading the Psalms, especially those that speak of trusting God in times of tribulation.

As the weeks passed, Lucia began to notice more significant changes. Obsessive thoughts lost their power. By focusing on prayer and God's presence, she found a safe haven for her mind. Her anxiety diminished, and her confidence began to return.

One afternoon, while walking in the park, Lucia stopped and looked around her. The trees, the blue sky, the birds singing—everything seemed more alive and beautiful. She felt deeply grateful and silently thanked God for the peace that filled her heart.

Sometime later, at a parish meeting, Lucia shared her story with other parishioners. She spoke of her struggle with obsessive thoughts and how prayer had transformed her life. "Prayer not only helped me find peace," she said, "but it also taught me to fully trust God. Every time I pray, I feel that I surrender my fears to someone much greater than myself, and that gives me an indescribable serenity."

Father Ildefonso, who was present at the meeting, smiled proudly. He knew that Lucia had found a path to healing and peace, and prayer had been the key that opened the door.

Lucia continued her daily prayer practice, always remembering Father Ilde-fonso's teachings. Her life was no longer dominated by anxiety and obsessive thoughts. She had found an anchor in prayer and a deep connection with the divine—a source of strength and serenity.

***

A 2004 study on prayer in the *Journal of Health Psychology* found that people who see God as a partner or collaborator in their lives or leave the solutions to their problems in God's hands have better mental and physical health outcomes. People who are angry with God—who feel punished or abandoned—have worse outcomes. The researchers also found that practicing prayer decreased anxiety and stress and generated a more positive mood.

Since the dawn of civilization, humankind has found solace in prayer. Throughout history, this practice has evolved and adapted to the beliefs and needs of each culture and religion.

From the starry nights of Mesopotamia, where the ancients knelt, whispering prayers to the heavens for protection and guidance, to Egypt, with its majestic pyramids and temples, prayer has always been a bridge between humans and their gods. In Greece, philosophers and citizens offered prayers to the gods of Olympus, hoping their petitions would be heard from high.

In the life of Jesus and the early Christians, prayer was an essential form of communication with God, seeking guidance, strength and comfort. Jesus taught prayer both as a ritual and an intimate conversation with the Heavenly Father.

In the book of Matthew, we find a powerful message:

> "Ask, and it will be given to you; seek, and you will find; knock, and it will be opened to you. For everyone who asks receives; and he who seeks finds; and to him who knocks, it will be opened."
>
> Matthew 7:7-8.

In the book of John, we read:

> "And whatever you ask in my name, I will do it, so that the Father may be glorified in the Son."
>
> John 14:13.

Mark reveals to us:

Therefore I tell you, whatever you ask for in prayer, believe that you have received it, and it will be yours.

Mark 11:24.

The ancient sages left us keys to activate the power of life, but in our fast-paced and chaotic world, we often forget what is really happening.

You are about to learn the most effective way to pray—to ask the universe for help. Pay close attention because you are about to discover one of the most powerful teachings in human history. This ancient wisdom will reveal how to activate the creative power within you. Open your mind and heart because this knowledge has the potential to transform your life in ways you never imagined.

First, you have to understand that you must be like a child: play, be happy and expect miracles with innocence and wonder. Jesus of Nazareth said that only children will enter the kingdom of heaven because they possess a purity that allows them to connect with the divine. Children have their third eye and pineal gland wide open, which gives them a perception beyond the physical. They maintain an intuitive connection with the source of creation. However, from the age of 12, the left brain hemisphere, the logical and rational one, begins to dominate. Gradually, the magic of childhood fades, and the mind becomes more rigid and limited. But you have the power to reconnect with that childlike essence and unlock your full potential again.

To pray, you must adopt the right mindset—one similar to that of a child: open, hopeful, and ready to receive miracles. While you can pray in any posture, kneeling shows humility and reverence, which enhances your spiritual connection. As you prostrate yourself before the divine presence, you acknowledge your smallness and dependence on God.

To relax, enter an alpha state, a state of mind where you can suggest anything to your subconscious. Breathing deeply and closing your eyes helps to enter this state.

Next, be clear about your desire and what you wish to manifest in the areas of health, money, or love. Ask God to intercede so that you can achieve it. Raise your prayers, knowing that you will be heard.

Visualize yourself enjoying that desired reality. Visualize briefly that you already have what you have asked for and that you enjoy it fully. Recreate in your mind every detail, every sensation associated with that reality. Remember the chapter on psychic visualization? Apply those principles now and allow your imagination to transport you to that ideal scenario. Feel the joy, fulfillment and peace that come over you as you see your dream come true. Let every cell in your body vibrate with the excitement of living what you have longed for.

Be grateful in advance for all that you have received, with the certainty that it is already yours. Whether you address God, the universe or divinity, do so with a heart overflowing with appreciation and recognition for the blessings you have received. With absolute assurance, affirm, "Thank you, Father. It is done. So it is, and so it shall be."

But remember, in praying, you leave the outcome of your request in the hands of God, in His infinite Wisdom. Be assured that He knows what is best for you. It may even be that what you ask for is not what is best for you at this time in your life. God will always give you what you need for your evolution and growth.

So ask with an open heart, but leave everything to those who know more than you. Let go of attachment to the outcome and trust in God's plan for your life. Keep your faith unwavering, knowing that your prayers will be answered in the perfect way and at the perfect time. Everything always happens for your highest good.

Finish the prayer by letting Divine Intelligence guide your requests so they are "in harmony with the divine will." This ensures that your desire does not conflict with others, is aligned with your purpose and comes as a perfect gift from heaven.

Trust that the universe knows what is best for you and everyone involved. Surrender your longings, knowing that they will be manifested in the perfect way and at the right time. The universe conspires in your favor when your requests align with the greater good.

If you want to know how scientific prayer works, you must understand that your emotion fertilizes your thinking in the quantum field. The combination of crystalline, clear and focused thought, along with intense, heightened and positive emotion, creates a powerful electromagnetic wave that sends a signal to the universe, and the universe will inevitably respond by attracting into your life that which you have imagined with such passion and clarity or that which you need.

There is an intelligence that is beyond your comprehension and reach, and it is at work right here and now. It is that intelligence that holds the whole cosmos together, that acts as the womb of creation. It is in the womb of this intelligence that all creation happens. And here's the key: you are allowed access to this intelligence. It is not blocked. It's simply that you've never looked there.

You are so absorbed in the small nature of what you are: your body, your thoughts, your emotions, your hormones. These things have occupied you so much that you have never stopped looking up or paying attention to something beyond yourself. You have been led to believe that you are a limited being, confined to the borders of your own skin. But this is a trap, a veil that hides your true nature. This is what we call Maya.

But here is the revelation: if you learn to look beyond these distractions, if you connect with that supreme intelligence, your life will be magically transformed. All you need to do is lift your gaze and show gratitude. In doing so, you will open the doors to a life full of blessings and wonders.

I assure you, with total conviction, that this process works infallibly. See for yourself and witness the magic your mind can create when you focus it with clarity and energy.

Practice this every day, especially before you surrender to the arms of Morpheus, and you will be amazed at how your life transforms in ways you never imagined.

Tool: Praying

MODULE II

ENERGY

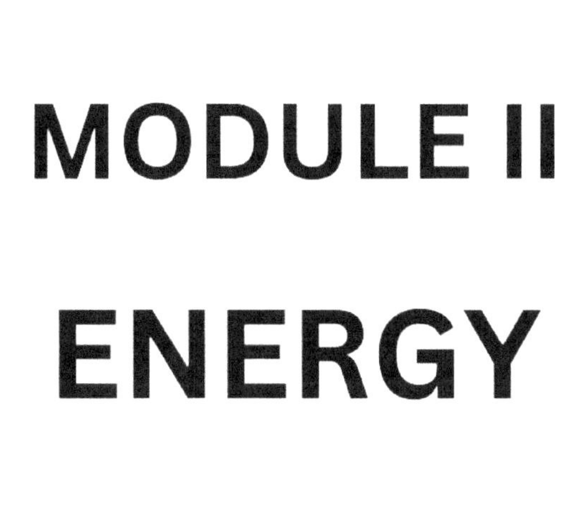

CHAPTER 1
Foundations

You Need Willpower

AFTER THE JOURNEY YOU have made through Module I, through which you have settled the necessary knowledge to transform your life, now it is time to dive into Module II, the DOING, the putting into practice what you have learned. It is time to put into action everything you have discovered about yourself and how to overcome anxiety and negative thoughts. All the theory is useless if you don't put it into practice. On the contrary, even if you put into action a small part of what you have learned, it would have been worth it.

Your path to success and happiness is deeply related to your willpower and your commitment to the goals you set. A strong and determined will that drives you to act. You must stay focused on what you want to achieve, not allowing obstacles or setbacks to discourage you. Every step you take, no matter how small, brings you closer to your goals.

Don't listen to those who say that willpower is not necessary. They do not understand the immense power that resides within you. Cultivate discipline and perseverance, for they will be your best allies in this journey. Your determination will be the key to reaching the pinnacle of success and experiencing the true happiness you deserve.

You need the willpower to put into practice the fabulous and motivating ideas you have decided to carry out. You will start with enthusiasm and motivation, but it is likely that one day, you will not feel energetic enough to do the exercises or use the tools in the book. When this happens to you, imagine the satisfaction you will feel when your dreams come true. Let that sense of accomplishment wash over you and keep you going, especially in times of sluggishness.

Don't let a temporary lack of motivation sidetrack you from your path to success and happiness. Keep the flame of your determination alive, and be confident in your ability to overcome any obstacle. Your willpower is the engine that will propel you forward, even on the most challenging days.

No matter how you feel, just do it, even if it costs you a little more. You will see the magic of doing it this way: your energy levels will rise, and it will get easier to do the exercises.

Through a fascinating process of resonance between the different levels that make up your being, any action on one of them automatically reflects on all the others. That is to say, if you behave as a person with great energy and an iron will, on the most material and tangible level, you will activate energetic channels that will make large amounts of energy existing on higher levels available to you.

You will notice how your motivation increases gradually, and your drive to continue becomes stronger. You will find that the more you persist, the easier it becomes to stay the course. Soon, you will be able to look back with pride and see how far you have come, thanks to your effort and perseverance.

Herein lies the immense value of discipline, of being able to do what you set out to do, even when you don't feel like it. Developing the willpower to do what you know you should do, even though part of you would rather be doing something else, is a skill that will open many doors for you. You will find that you can achieve great and extraordinary things in your life if you just strive to slightly increase your levels of self-discipline day by day.

It's not about becoming a completely different person overnight but about taking small steps in the right direction. Those small habits and routines that you incorporate, even if they seem insignificant at first, will accumulate and take you a long way.

Remember what you have read in previous chapters about the great value of repetition in establishing both a skill and a new habit. Don't be discouraged; a great journey always starts with small steps. But you must take them.

Everything I propose in this book will only be useful for you if you act and carry it out with your will and discipline.

You Are Responsible for Your Life

You are responsible for what happens in your life much more than you think. You can no longer blame circumstances, other people or chance for your current situation. It is time for you to take control, stop making excuses and take charge of your own destiny. Only you have the power to change things, make different decisions, and forge the future you want. Accept that power, use it wisely, and you will see how, little by little, things begin to change for the better.

Erase from your mind the idea that you are a victim of circumstances. Banish that limiting thought that things happen to you and you have no control over them. This is a negative mental habit that does nothing to help you succeed in the ventures you want to undertake. It keeps you paralyzed, robs you of power and undermines your confidence. Instead of seeing yourself as a helpless victim, realize that you have the ability to influence your reality with your decisions and actions.

You may have experienced triggering or unfair situations that have pushed you in a certain direction, storms that have blown you off course, but you always have the choice to take the rudder back into your hands and steer the ship in the right direction. No matter how hard the wind has blown against you or how big the waves have been that threatened to sink you, you will always have the power to choose how you respond and where you want to go from here. So, take control, adjust your sails and set your course toward your dreams and goals. The ocean of life can be unpredictable, but with determination and a positive attitude, you will get there.

Whether you are a man and blame women—or you're a woman and blame men—for the fact that your emotional and sexual relationships are not going well, it is time to ask yourself: what are you going to do to improve your relationships? Are you trying to change the men and women you relate to? That is not the solution.

You cannot change others, but you can change your own ways of thinking and acting. Through this internal change, you will see your new positive attitudes reflected in your relationships. Take responsibility for working on yourself, your thoughts and your behaviors. Observe how you react to certain situations and people and ask yourself if those reactions are helping you build satisfying relationships. If not, it's time to make some adjustments. Change starts from within. As you transform your inner world, you will see your outer world, including your relationships, transform for the better as well.

The Hermetic Principle of Correspondence says, "As within so without." This means that your outer world is largely a reflection of your inner world, that is, your thoughts, emotions and actions. What you experience in your relationships and in your life, in general, is directly related to what is happening inside you.

If you want to see positive changes in your external reality, you must begin by working on your internal reality. Cultivate thoughts of love, compassion and gratitude. Manage your emotions in a healthy way. Take actions aligned with your values and goals. As you transform your inner self, you will see how your outer world will also transform to reflect the new positive energy you are emanating.

Even though you may not have control over other people's actions or situations that come to you from the outside, you do have control over how you react to them. You are the master of your thoughts and emotions. You have the power to choose how to respond in every situation rather than simply reacting automatically.

Stop being a victim of your circumstances and take responsibility for your life. Take charge and consciously decide how you want to feel and act, regardless of what is happening around you. Remember, your happiness and inner peace do not depend on external factors but on your attitude and inner perspective.

So, take the bull by the horns and decide to change the things you can change within yourself. Don't let your fears paralyze you. Decide to be the protagonist and scriptwriter of the movie of your life instead of being a passive spectator carried away by circumstances. You have the power to write your own script and choose your thoughts, reactions, and actions. Take advantage of your innate ability to direct the course of your existence. You are the author of your story, so make sure you create an exciting and satisfying plot.

Choose Your Thoughts and Beliefs Carefully

Here are some examples of limiting beliefs and thoughts that I recommend you let go of:

I Can't Be Totally Happy Because Something Always Goes Wrong

Happiness is a state of mind that you can cultivate, even when facing life challenges. Don't let setbacks keep you from enjoying the good times. Learn to focus on the positive aspects of every situation and find joy and gratitude in the little everyday things. Celebrate your accomplishments, no matter how small.

Life is Hard

There is no doubt about it. There will be times when you feel that everything is stacked against you and the obstacles are insurmountable. However, you mustn't let these setbacks keep you from enjoying the good times.

Showing Emotions is for Weak People

Expressing emotions is a sign of strength and authenticity. Don't be afraid to show your human side. Allow yourself to feel the full spectrum of emotions, from joy and love to sadness and anger. Share your feelings with those you trust, as this will allow you to create deeper bonds.

Opportunity Knocks Only Once

Opportunities are constantly around you, waiting for you to discover and seize them. Keep an open mind and a positive attitude to recognize them when they come your way. Don't be discouraged if some doors close; new ones will open.

I Have No Control Over My Life

You have more control than you think. Make conscious decisions and focus on what you can change. Attitude and perspective play a crucial role in how you manage your life. Don't let negative thoughts and limiting beliefs make you feel powerless. Instead, recognize your ability to influence your environment and your future. Choose thoughts that empower you and motivate you to act. Set goals and work on achieving them.

I Don't Deserve It

We all deserve love, success and happiness. Believe in your worth and your ability to achieve your dreams. You are a valuable person and worthy of love. Recognize your talents. Embrace your talents and allow yourself to shine. Remember that you deserve to achieve happiness and success in all areas of your life.

No One Loves Me

You are worthy of love and affection; never doubt it. Sometimes, the most important love starts with yourself. Learn to cultivate self-love, treat yourself with compassion and recognize your inherent worth. Surround yourself with people who truly appreciate you, celebrate your triumphs and support you in difficult times. Open your heart to those who respect and value you for who you are.

I Can't

You can achieve more than you imagine. Eliminate 'I can't' from your vocabulary and replace it with 'I can try' or 'How can I make it happen? Don't give up in the face of difficulties; face them with courage and determination. Believe in yourself and your abilities. Persistence is the key to achieving your most ambitious goals.

It is Impossible

Many things that once seemed impossible are now reality. Don't be limited by what others say or what you have believed in the past. Keep an open mind and be willing to explore new possibilities. Every day is an opportunity to learn, grow and overcome obstacles.

By letting go of these limiting beliefs, you open the door to a fuller, happier and more successful life. The future is full of possibilities!

Instead, embrace empowering beliefs such as:

I Create My Destiny

You have the power to influence your life with your decisions and actions. Every step you take leads you toward your desired future. You are the architect of your own destiny. With every thought you choose, every belief you adopt and every action you take, you are shaping the direction of your life.

No One Can Hurt Me If I Don't Allow It

You control your emotions and reactions. Don't let the actions or words of others define your happiness. You have the power to choose positive thoughts and focus on your inner well-being, regardless of external circumstances. Remember, your peace of mind and self-esteem do not depend on the approval or behavior of others. You own your feelings and have the ability to cultivate serenity and joy from within yourself. Don't cede that power to anyone else.

Life is Wonderful!

Focus on the opportunities that life offers you. Cultivate a sense of gratitude for all the blessings, big and small, that fill your days. Marvel at the beauty of the world around you, from a spectacular sunrise to the warm smile of a loved one. Actively seek out reasons to feel grateful and watch how this optimistic perspective transforms your daily experience.

Everything Happens for a Reason

Trust that everything has a purpose. Learn from every situation and use it as an opportunity to grow and improve. Choose to see possibilities even in challenges, knowing that every obstacle brings valuable lessons and opportunities for growth. You may be guided onto a new path that will turn out to be much better than you imagined. The universe is working in your favor, even in ways you can't yet understand.

Everything Is Going to Be All Right

Remain calm and confident, even in difficult times. Breathe deeply, focus your thoughts on the positive and visualize a favorable outcome. Remain firm in your conviction that everything is going to work out, and it will.

I Can Do It!

Believe in your abilities and your capacity to achieve your goals. Trust in yourself and all that you are capable of achieving.

Adopting these empowering beliefs transforms your mindset and opens a path to a happier and more successful life. Believe in yourself and your ability to create the life you desire. The power is in your hands!

CHAPTER 2
The Roadmap

IMAGINE FOR A MOMENT that you are in a completely dark room. You can't see anything around you. You feel disoriented, confused and maybe even scared. This darkness is a perfect metaphor for the stress and anxiety that surrounds you. However, there is a way out, and you have the tools to find it in your hands: flashlights. Those flashlights represent each of the insights and tools you have discovered in this book. Each healthy habit you adopt is like lighting a new lantern in your life. Each exercise you practice, each strategy you implement, becomes a beam of light that dispels the darkness of anxiety and overthinking.

Imagine lighting your first flashlight by getting into the habit of walking two hours a day in nature. At first, the light is dim, but as this habit settles in, the flashlight shines brighter into the room. Each walk in the park or nearby forest reduces your anxiety and envelops you in a sense of calm.

You decide, then, to start a physical exercise program three days a week. As you do so, you turn on a second flashlight that adds to the first, further illuminating your room. Two flashlights are now lit. Each workout strengthens your body and clears your mind. The room, once dark and scary, now begins to light up.

A little later, you incorporate daily breathing exercises. These not only complement your physical routine but become your anchor in times of anxiety. It's like turning on an additional third big flashlight, dispelling the shadows of negative thoughts and filling the room with light and calm.

Later, you decide to start using the **"Act as if You Already Have It"** tool five minutes daily. Another lighted flashlight shines into your room.

Little by little, with each new flashlight you turn on, the darkness disappears. The room gets brighter and brighter. It is a gradual process, but with dedication and persistence, the room will be completely illuminated, and you will be able to see everything from a renewed perspective.

The secret to freeing yourself from anxiety lies in turning on as many flashlights as possible to light up the room and in establishing as many anti-anxiety habits in your life as possible. This will require effort and discipline in the beginning. You will need to consistently practice new ways of thinking and acting until they become an integral part of your daily routine. Over time, these positive habits will be put on autopilot, becoming natural and spontaneous for you.

Remember, every flashlight you turn on not only illuminates your path but also strengthens you. The more you learn and adopt healthy habits, the brighter the light that will guide you. Keep going, keep learning and keep growing. Turn on flashlight after flashlight until your life is fully illuminated with the light of your progress and peace of mind.

Until now, the only thing that has prevented you from reaching your goals has been the lack of knowledge and necessary tools. Now, you have in your hands the keys that open the door to a life free of anxiety. With each exercise you practice, you will empower yourself to overcome obstacles and move forward with determination toward what you desire.

Start today, turn on your first flashlight and walk confidently towards a life free of stress and anxiety! Your well-being is at your fingertips. Don't settle for darkness when you can light up your life with every little habit you adopt.

CHAPTER 3

The Secret of the Double Habit

Jorge had always dreamed of being a public speaker. He admired those who could stand up in front of a crowd and speak with confidence. However, every time he tried to do so, a paralyzing fear would grip him. His palms would sweat, his heart would pound, and his mind would cloud over. He needed a solution to overcome this fear and transform his life.

One day, while attending a personal development workshop, Jorge listened to a speaker discussing the power of body behavior to change emotions. *She mentioned a technique called the "Double Habit," which involved replacing a negative habit with an immediate positive behavior. Intrigued, Jorge approached her after the seminar and asked for more details.*

The speaker, whose name was Laura, explained him that he could use his body to change his emotional state. When he feels fear, instead of giving in to anxiety, he should adopt a power posture, such as raising his arms in victory or standing with his feet firmly planted and his shoulders back. This simple physical act could transform his fear into courage.

That night, Jorge decided to put what he had learned into practice. He knew that his habit of slouching and looking down whenever he felt afraid only made his anxiety worse. Instead, he thought of a power pose he could easily adopt. He decided that every time he felt fear, he would raise his arms in victory and take a deep breath.

The next morning, Jorge was preparing for an important meeting at work. He felt the familiar knot in his stomach and sweaty palms. But this time, instead of slouching, he remembered his plan. He raised his arms in victory and took a deep breath. He noticed how his heart began to calm down, and his mind cleared.

Throughout the day, whenever he felt fear approaching, Jorge adopted his power stance. To his surprise, not only did he feel less anxious, but he also felt braver and more confident. At the end of the day, he reflected on how this simple change in his body behavior had had such a big impact.

As the weeks went on, Jorge began to incorporate more empowering behaviors into his daily life. In addition to raising his arms in victory, he began to walk with his shoulders back and head held high whenever he felt nervous. The Double Habit technique not only reduced his fear but also gave him a sense of control and empowerment.

One day, while giving his first public talk, Jorge felt nervous. But instead of giving in to the fear, he raised his arms in victory before taking the stage. The audience cheered, and for the first time, he felt the courage to follow his dream.

***

Jorge's story is a testament to the transformative power of the *double habit* combined with the *"act as if" tool*. By replacing fear with empowered postures, Jorge discovered a new way to live and face his fears. You can do it too. Identify your moments of fear, choose a power posture you can easily adopt and start replacing them today. Courage and confidence are within your reach.

Habits are a fundamental part of your identity. What you do on a regular basis makes up a large part of your daily activities. In fact, it is estimated that up to 70% of your conscious behavior is made up of habits. These automated patterns of behavior largely determine who you are and how you function in the world. Your routines, from the moment you wake up to the moment you go to bed, are shaped by the habits you have developed over time.

Forming a habit is a variable process. Some say it takes 21 days, some say 18 days, some say 30 days, and some say it takes up to 60 days. So, what's the truth?

A study published in 2010 by Lally found that, for the same habit, it can take anywhere from 18 to 254 days for different individuals. So, if you've been discouraged because you haven't formed a habit in 21 days, don't worry; it's completely normal! Don't compare yourself to others or put too much pressure on yourself.

Science has provided us with valuable tools to understand how the nervous system learns and adapts. The key is neuroplasticity, the brain's ability to reorganize itself and form new neural connections.

Sometimes, it's about simply forming new habits, but it can also come down to the fact that you want to eliminate habits that don't do you much good. Breaking a bad habit may seem like a Herculean task, but there is a surprisingly simple and powerful secret: inhibiting it is not enough. To get rid of a bad habit, you must immediately replace it with a positive behavior.

This technique, known as the *"double habit,"* is key to transforming your life. The double habit is that the moment you feel the urge to fall into your bad habit, you immediately replace it with a positive action. It's not just about interrupting the cycle of the bad habit but introducing a beneficial behavior.

For example, you're at your desk, trying to concentrate on an important task, but your hand slips to your phone without realizing it. Before you know it, you're checking social media and wasting valuable minutes. Instead of simply putting down your phone, which can be difficult and frustrating, here's a different approach.

Tool: How to Eliminate a Negative Habit

Here is the detailed process:

1. Identify the Bad Habit

First, identify the bad habit you want to change. In this case, it's checking your phone in an exaggerated way. The key is to be aware of the moment when you are about to fall into that unwanted behavior.

2. Plan the Positive Replacement

The next step is to have a positive behavior ready to replace the bad habit. It can be something as simple as stretching, touching your ear, or drinking a glass of water. The key is that this action should be easy to do and accessible in the moment.

3. Execute the Replacement Immediately

Whenever you find yourself checking your phone, instead of just putting it down, perform your positive action immediately. For example, if you notice that you are unlocking your phone, stop and drink a glass of water. This immediate action not only breaks the cycle of the bad habit but also provides you with a tangible benefit, such as being more hydrated.

4. Coat the New Neural Circuitry with Myelin

Over time, your brain will begin to associate the impulse to check your phone with the new positive behavior. You're creating a new neural pathway that replaces the old habit with a new, beneficial one.

The Science Behind the Double Habit

According to Hermetic Science, this is the key to the "double habit." Instead of simply trying to eliminate the unwanted habit, you use its own power to rewrite a new, positive pattern over it. In effect, you are channeling the energy of the old habit and redirecting it to feed the new one.

When you perform a positive behavior immediately after feeling the urge to engage in a bad habit, you take advantage of a crucial moment when the neurons responsible for the bad habit are still active and receptive to change.

By introducing a new behavior at this precise instant, you begin to gradually "dismantle" the neural circuits associated with the bad habit, gradually weakening the connections that support it. At the same time, you are building and strengthening new neural circuits for the positive behavior you have chosen.

With each conscious repetition, you are shaping your brain to favor the new habit over the old one, creating a new neural pathway that will eventually become automatic and natural for you.

This approach is not only effective for habits like checking your phone but can be applied to any bad habit you want to change. Whether you want to stop overeating, procrastinating or any other unwanted behavior, the dual habit is a powerful tool for change.

Breaking a bad habit doesn't have to be a never-ending battle. With the dual-habit approach, you can transform your behaviors and create a more productive and healthy life. Remember, the key is to replace the bad habit with an immediate positive action.

Start today, identify your bad habits, plan your positive replacements and watch your life begin to change for the better!

Call To Action

Write down on a piece of paper three habits that contribute to raising your anxiety level. Perhaps you notice patterns like procrastinating on important tasks, obsessively checking social media, or skipping healthy meals. Choose one of those habits and commit to using the double habit technique. Plan a specific positive replacement that you can do immediately whenever you catch yourself falling into that bad habit.

Habit 1

Habit 2.

Habit 3.

Keep track of your progress and celebrate each small victory on the road to creating healthier habits. Remember, you have the power to transform your life, one habit at a time.

Don't limit yourself to simply stopping doing what you don't want. Instead, start doing something that actually benefits you. The power is in your hands!

CHAPTER 4
Weekly Habit Tracker

Instructions:

- Select the habits or tools you wish to perform this week.

- Check off each day that you complete the habit.

- Be sure to complete the required exercises at least the minimum number of times.

- Add up the points at the end of the week and review your progress.

Minimum Essential Exercises:

Conscious Breathing: At least 5 times per week

Alternate Breathing: At least 3 times per week

Basic Relaxing Breathing: At least 4 times per week

Cardiovascular Exercise (moderate): At least 3 times per week

Cardiovascular Exercise (intense): At least 2 times per week

How to use the chart:

Customize the Habits: Add or remove habits according to your preferences and needs.

Plan your Week: Before the week begins, decide which habits you want to practice each day and write down the points.

Track Your Progress: Use a symbol, such as a checkmark (✓), to indicate the days you completed the habit and add up the points at the end of each day.

Reflect and Adjust: At the end of the week, reflect on your progress. What worked well? What could be improved? Adjust your goals for the next week accordingly.

WEEKLY SCHEDULE

HABITS & TOOLS	M	T	W	T	F	S	S
PRETEND, ACT AS IF							
CONSCIOUS BREATHING							
ALTERNATE BREATHING							
BHRAMARI PRANAYAMA							
BREATH OF URGENCY							
MODERATE CARDIO SESSION							
INTENSE CARDIO SESSION							
STRENGTH TRAINING							
YOGA							
KARATE/KUNG FU							
PILATES							
TAI CHI/QI GONG							
DANCE							
RECSPORTS: SOCCER, TENNIS, ETC							

PLANNING HEBDOMADAIRE

HABITUDES ET OUTILS	L	M	M	J	V	S	D
AGIS COMME SI							
RESPIRATION CONSCIENTE							
RESPIRATION ALTERNÉE							
RESPIRATION ANTI-STRESS							
RESPIRATION D'URGENCE							
SÉANCE CARDIO MODÉRÉE							
SÉANCE CARDIO INTENSE							
ENTRAÎNEMENT DE FORCE							
YOGA							
KARATÉ/KUNG-FU							
PILATES							
TAI-CHI/QI-GONG							
DANSE							
SPORT SOCIAUX : TENNIS/ETC							

NOTES

WEEKLY SCHEDULE

HABITS & TOOLS	M	T	W	T	F	S	S
ART THERAPY EXERCISE 1							
ART THERAPY EXERCISE 2							
ART THERAPY EXERCISE 3							
BODY RELAXATION EXERCISE							
MEDITATION 1							
MEDITATION 2							
MINDFULNESS							
BOOK READING							
CREATIVE VISUALIZATION							
MUSIC THERAPY							
DO SOMETHING GOOD FOR OTHERS							
PRAYER							

WEEKLY SCHEDULE

HABITS & TOOLS	M	T	W	T	F	S	S

Farewell

Congratulations! If you've made it this far, I want to congratulate you on your dedication and commitment. It is not easy to face and understand anxiety, but you have taken a big step towards a calmer and more conscious life. I sincerely hope that what you have learned in this book will be of great use to you in your fight against anxiety.

In addition, I want to inform you that I have created a specially designed workbook or activity book to support everything you have learned in this book. This additional resource will help you to apply in a practical way the strategies and knowledge acquired, strengthening your path toward a freer and more peaceful mind.

Always remember that every little advance counts and that you have within you the strength to overcome any challenge. Go forward with confidence and perseverance. I wish you every success on your path to a life without anxiety!

With all my support and best wishes.

Jesus Cediel.

About The Author

Jesús Cediel is an independent researcher with over 40 years of experience in hypnosis, mental processes, and the exploration of human consciousness. His captivating journey began at the age of fourteen, when he delved into the worlds of astrology and hypnosis, setting the foundation for a life dedicated to uncovering the deepest mysteries of human existence.

Driven by an insatiable curiosity, Jesús Cediel has explored an impressive array of disciplines, including martial arts, hermeticism, orientalism, sacred sexuality, anti-aging medicine, and natural therapies. Yet, his greatest spiritual passion lies in the comparative study of ancient religions and mythologies, a pursuit that has allowed him to weave together threads of wisdom from cultures across time.

With a multidisciplinary perspective and a unique vision, Jesús Cediel brings extraordinary depth to his work, offering fresh insights into timeless philosophical questions and guiding his readers toward a deeper understanding of the mind and spirit.

www.ingramcontent.com/pod-product-compliance
Lightning Source LLC
Chambersburg PA
CBHW051553250726
48653CB00004BA/1133